Bereavement
Counseling
IN THE
SCHOOL
SETTING

Luciano Sabatini

Published by WriteLife, LLC
2323 S. 171 St.
Suite 202
Omaha, NE 68130
www.writelife.com

in cooperation with

Grief Illustrated Press
PO Box 4600
Omaha, NE 68104
www.centering.org

Printed in the United States of America

ISBN 978 1 60808 072 4

First Edition

ACKNOWLEDGEMENTS

To my loving and supportive family, my wife Suzanne and
my children Kara, Craig and Nina who have given me a sense of
purpose and fulfillment, and brought great joy to my life.

To the many adolescents who I have had the privilege of working
with and who inspired me to write this book, they have taught me
so much about life, loss and dealing with adversity.

To my late wife Linda, may she always be at peace knowing
that her tragic death started me on a journey in which
I was able to help so many.

TABLE OF CONTENTS

INTRODUCTION

In my 37 years as an educator, I was fortunate to work for several different schools or school districts in differing roles such as teacher, athletic coach, school counselor, guidance department chairman, and director of guidance. While I admit that I did not enjoy all aspects of my jobs, there were other activities that I developed a great passion for, and they gave great meaning to my work. The most significant of these was to facilitate a support group each year for students who had lost a family member. This was an outgrowth of my work as a bereavement counselor. In my support groups and private counseling sessions with newly bereaved adults, I would frequently hear the frustration of parents who were trying to assist their children in coping with the loss of a parent or sibling. In most cases, the parents did not understand that young children and teens grieve very differently than adults.

This gave me the impetus to reach out to the students who had lost a family member. For 15 years, I facilitated an adolescent support group, which usually started at the end of November. It met through the holiday period and often into the spring. I admired these youngsters who often felt isolated and stigmatized by peers and adults who did not understand them and were not sensitive to their needs. The resiliency and maturity that many of them showed in facing life without a parent or other family member was remarkable. Conversely, it was sad to see some who struggled with issues related to unresolved grief because family and friends seemed unable to offer the support that they needed.

This book is written for them in the hope that we can better provide for their needs. In the pages that follow, I have taken what I have learned from them and tried to share it with the reader in a practical way that can be used in a school setting. It is my hope that this book will serve as a resource for school mental health professionals, such as counselors, social workers, and psychologists to assist them in their work with these students. Teachers, administrators, and other staff will find this book valuable as well.

WHY THIS BOOK

In the United States, more than 2 million children and adolescents (3.4%) younger than 18 years of age have experienced the death of a parent. This does not include the loss of a sibling, step parent or other members of the household. This means that in the typical classroom chances are that one or two students have suffered the loss of a close family member. Oftentimes, unless the death occurred fairly recently, the teachers, counselors and administration may not even know of the loss. Consequently, they are often overlooked as schools address more high profile concerns.

Our schools have developed curricula over the years to address serious challenges faced by adolescents such as substance abuse and drinking while driving. Through special assemblies, health education classes and student service clubs like SADD, students are much more sensitized to the dangers of driving while intoxicated. In the 1980's, the AIDS epidemic fostered a plethora of school based programs educating students on how to protect themselves from being infected with the HIV virus. Most recently, with the highly publicized suicides of victims of bullying, schools are developing anti-bullying curricula or programs that can be taught in schools to assist vulnerable students. While these are all commendable efforts, no such comparable action has been taken to assist students with the one common denominator that we all face, death.

Our death-phobic society has avoided introducing death

education to our elementary, middle, or high school curriculum. Death is not a popular topic and runs counter to our youth-oriented and self-indulgent emphasis. Therefore, the adults in our society have grown up illiterate on issues dealing with death and grief, and often say the wrong things or do not take the best course of action on behalf of her children.

Many students in my support groups have reported how well-meaning parents tried to protect them by not being truthful regarding the declining health of a family member. These students knew that something was seriously wrong but had to live with the secrecy that parents felt would protect them. Other students reported how they were forced to attend counseling after the death of a parent because adult family members felt that they were not grieving in the right way. In my own experiences, some parents felt threatened when their child expressed an interest in joining a support group. In their view, having the adolescent talk about their loss and hearing about the grief of others, would release tumultuous feelings that would cause irrevocable harm. Perhaps the saddest cases were students who lost a parent when they were very young. The surviving parent often remarries and the new couple feels threatened by the child's normal preoccupation to learn about the deceased parent.

Clearly, the best long term solution for our children is the creation of curricula on death education which can be incorporated into a class, preferably in upper elementary or middle school. Some faith-based schools currently teach death education as part of their religious education. By having a death education curriculum, the topic becomes part of the students' educational process and death becomes normalized rather than demonized. However, until our society overcomes its death phobia, we need a short term solution to help those youngsters who have lost a parent and the many others who have lost siblings or other loved ones.

Support groups can be a very effective tool in assisting these students. Students who have lived through a painful and life-altering loss have a lot to share with each other. The group gives them the opportunity to compare their thoughts and feelings, and sometimes gain new perspective on their loss. With trained leaders, they can review misconceptions and misguided suggestions made by well-meaning but death illiterate adults.

The most important reason for writing this book is that we owe some assistance to these students. They are victims of a society that would prefer not to be reminded of something that we all fear, death. Consequently, these students often grow up with unresolved issues, unanswered questions, and for some a misguided sense of responsibility or guilt for the death of the loved one. They become adults who relive the painful experience of an unresolved loss each time a significant person in their life dies. The unfinished business becomes a weight that impedes a more fulfilling life. Studies have shown that individuals who have suffered major losses in their lives are more predisposed to mental illness.

Colin Murray Parkes conducted a study of 3,245 patients admitted into two psychiatric units during a six year period of time. Ninety-four of these had suffered a major loss (parent, spouse, sibling or child) within the past six months. This ratio of bereaved to patient population was much higher than the ratio of bereaved to the normal population. Therefore, a link between mental illness and bereavement seems to be indicated. Psychiatrists treating the patients found that the bereaved patients differed from the others in two important respects. The bereaved patients had been diagnosed as suffering from many different types of psychiatric illness and second that the most common single diagnosis in this group was reactive or neurotic depression. This was the diagnosis for 28% of the bereaved patients and only 15% of patients who had not been bereaved[1]

Finally, the death of a student can be one of the most devastating experiences in the life of a school. It is a very challenging time which requires leaders who are well versed in crisis intervention strategies.

The final two chapters seek to offer some practices and procedures learned from real life experiences that would help the school in managing the crisis.

THE NATURE OF GRIEF

Before we can begin to discuss how to assist students with death of a loved one, there is basic information that mental health professionals in a school setting must know about the nature of grief. Grief has been a part of our evolutionary past and has biological origins. John Bowlby wrote extensively on attachment theory. Affectional bonds between young animals and their mothers have survival value. For example, when the young animal becomes separated from its mother, behavior that we associate with grieving such as crying, fear, searching, and angry outbursts are instinctively triggered to reunite the young animal with its mother. Similarly, a human child will use the same behaviors when he is lost and trying to find his mother.

Konrad Lorenz observed grief among geese. One of the most common grief reactions is searching behavior. He observed the following behavior in a graylag goose upon losing its mate.

The first response to the disappearance of the partner consists of an anxious attempt to find him again. The goose moves about restlessly by day and night, flying great distances and visiting places where the partner may be found, uttering all the time the penetrating trisyllabic long-distance call. The searching expeditions are extended farther and farther and quite often the searcher gets lost, or succumbs to an accident. All the objective observable characteristics of the goose's behavior on losing its mate are roughly identical with human grief. [2]

Newly bereaved people will experience this searching instinct even while knowing that the person has died. There are many other similar observations that have been made from the animal kingdom. Dog owners commonly report sadness, searching, and other grieving behaviors that the animal exhibits upon the death of a family member.

While we still carry instinctual grief reactions as part of our evolutionary past, few would doubt that cultural influences and psychological factors play a much more important role in how we experience grief today. Freud was one of the first to propose a model to explain the psychodynamics of grief. According to Freud, when we lose a loved one, the loss is too powerful to accept immediately. Therefore, the newly bereaved creates an Introject or internal image, of the loved one. At first the image is very strong, but with the passage of time the mourner begins to slowly withdraw her emotional bonds from the deceased and begins to reinvest this emotional energy into someone or something else. As this process continues, the Introject begins to fade until decathexis, the severing of all emotional ties with the deceased, takes place. The concept of decathexis has been disputed by prominent scholars in the field of bereavement counseling who claim that emotional ties are never severed but rather the survivor maintains some emotional connection with the deceased. According to William Worden, the survivor needs to find an enduring connection with the deceased in the midst of embarking on a new life. The emotional bonds can be very healthy as long as they are relegated to a person's past and not part of the present or future. Another important component of grief is that it is a process where the individual goes through a series of cognitive and affective changes as healing takes place. Kubler-Ross developed one of the first models to explain this process. In her work with the terminally ill, she identified five stages of dying: denial, rage and anger, bargaining, depression, and acceptance. In each stage an individual confronts a new set of feelings and thoughts which when successfully resolved leads to the next stage. Eventually, the terminally ill reach a level of peace and acceptance. Kubler-Ross later adapted this model to explain the grief process with the newly bereaved. Some mental health practitioners found her model to be too rigid since for most individuals the stages were fluid. Feelings and thoughts did not proceed in such a linear, sequential order as indicated by the model, but rather there was overlap and digression from one stage to another. In Stroebe's dual process model, she describes grief as a dynamic oscillating process where the focus of the individual alternates between the loss of the person (loss orientation) and moving beyond the loss (restoration orientation). This oscillation between two focal points is very different from Kubler-Ross' linear model. Colin Murray Parkes proposed a model based on a study he did with bereaved adults. He explained the grief process as occurring in phases, which is similar to the stages model. He followed a group of bereaved adults for two years and identified four phases in their healing process. The first phase is numbness which is a protective devise against the awful reality of the death. Then, the next phase is one of yearning where the mourner hopes to reunite with the deceased and even disregards or denies the permanence of death. In the third phase, the individual faces the reality of the death and goes through a period of disorganization and despair. It becomes very difficult for the bereaved to function in her daily living. In the last phase, the person begins to pull herself together and enters a period of reorganized behavior where she resumes a more normal level of functioning. Catherine Sanders also uses phases to describe the grief process but her model has five phases which include: shock, awareness of loss, conservation-withdrawal, healing, and renewal. These are all variations of the same fundamental concept that grief is a dynamic process which entails many affective and cognitive adjustments that the bereaved must make in the healing process.

Theorists have also identified tasks of grief which emphasize that healing from grief is an active process. Progressing through the stages/phases requires effort, also known as " grief work". William Worden prefers to focus on tasks in his work which eliminates some of the confusion and rigidity that is associated with stages/phases. The tasks of grief do not focus on order or sequence, but on tasks to be accomplished. In Worden's model, there are four tasks which include accepting the reality of the loss, processing the pain of grief, adjusting to a world without the deceased, and finding an enduring connection in the midst of embarking upon a new life.

Most recently, researchers such as Bonanno have questioned these paradigms on grief. He conducted interviews with hundreds of newly bereaved and found little evidence of stages/phases or tasks of grief. He also does not believe in the often used term "grief work". Bonanno believes that bereavement theorists and practitioners have underestimated the capacity for resilience among the newly bereaved. Based on our human experience, people are wired to deal with loss. He does not dispute that loss of a loved one is a very painful life event but the majority of people recover without the need for bereavement counseling. From his research, only about 10% to 15 % of people suffer from chronic grief reactions which would necessitate the need for therapeutic intervention.

From the perspective of the newly bereaved, what is their experience? Do they recognize the existence of stages, phases, tasks, or grief work? The newly bereaved would certainly acknowledge the existence of tremendous emotional and psychological upheaval following the loss of a loved one, but their highly enmeshed feelings and thoughts would be difficult to categorize into a model of grief. The models offer a framework that the mental health professional can use to assist the newly bereaved. Because of the very individualistic nature of grief, all of these models, including Bonanno's resilience theory, have some validity. While many individuals bounce back on their own, some who may have more complicated and intense grief reactions can benefit from the explanations provided by the models cited above.

In addition to the biological and psychological components of grief, the cultural and religious beliefs that we grew up with have a huge impact on how we grieve. Grief is a very individual experience and we learn about grief from our family. Our parent's attitudes, comfort level, and belief system regarding death will affect how we experience grief. In my work in schools, I have experienced this first hand. I once interviewed a Chinese student whose mother died. The student reported that the family reassured her that her mother's illness was not that serious and that she would be fine. A few days before her mother died, she was told the truth. While the student suspected that her mother's health was much worse than she was told, the news was devastating and she did not have much time to prepare for her mother's death. I was starting a support group which this student was interested in joining. However, when she asked her family for permission to join this group, they denied her request. In a follow-up interview with her, she told me that her family did not approve of her being part of such a group. In her culture, talking in such a group and revealing personal matters might bring shame to the family. Therefore, safeguarding the image of the family took priority over her individual needs. Although this was a very poignant example, cultural beliefs often get in the way of the individual receiving help. Also, in trying to protect the child by avoiding the truth, the family can hinder the grief process by preventing important discussions from taking place between the child and dying family member.

The Irish have a very different reaction to death. Monica McGoldrick writes about how important it is to Irish families that the deceased have "a proper sendoff" to the life beyond death. They make a point of attending all wakes and funerals of family members and friends, sparing no expense for drink or other arrangements, even if they have very little money. Even those who are estranged are expected to show up for wakes and funerals which can be important occasions for reconciliation.[3] The wake is a festive affair resembling a wedding with plenty to drink and eat as well as jokes and funny stories about the deceased. However, after the funeral, mourners tend to suffer in silence.

Irish family members are not expected to even mention the deceased. All are expected to move on with their lives without any kind of mourning period or support from other family members. This conspiracy of silence is going to make the Irish student less receptive to counseling from school mental health professionals.

For cultures with a very strong Catholic identity such as the Latinos and Italians, the belief in God's will and on the existence of an afterlife have a huge impact on their grieving process. According to their belief system, the deceased was taken from them because it was God's will. Followers of Catholicism are expected to accept that God had good reason for taking the deceased; it is not for us to know why but just to accept that God knows best. Furthermore, the newly bereaved are comforted knowing that they will be reunited with their loved one when they die. Therefore, the harsh reality of the permanence of death is to some degree mitigated by the belief of this eventual reunification. In my work as a bereavement counselor, I have been amazed at how Catholics with a very strong faith seem to experience less of the emotional and psychological turmoil of grief. Although the pain of grief is the same as others, they have fewer conflicts in terms of accepting the loss and they look forward to their reunification with the loved one after death. Conversely, I have also witnessed very religious Catholics who experience a crisis in faith in their grief process. They question why after being devout and good practicing Catholics all their lives, God should punish them by taking away the person that they love the most. In these cases, their grief is compounded with a sense of betrayal by a God that they worshipped all their lives. In my experience, adolescents are more often angry at God than accepting of his master plan, and resolving their anger is part of their grief work.

In some faiths there is more emphasis on the person's earthly life than an afterlife. In the Jewish faith, according to Petkov, the spotlight shines upon one's present life. According to Jewish tradition, our lives are measured by our deeds and whether we have lived up to our full potential. Death, then, allows us to value life and to live a life full of meaning. Jewish values emphasize strong family ties, personal achievement, financial success, and educational advancement. Jews tend to focus on life's accomplishments and successes rather than on what will happen when someone dies.[4] Jews are more apt to discuss the lives of their loved one, and are more open in counseling to discussing their thoughts and feelings. On the other hand, the permanence of death takes on a harsher reality because there is no clear belief in a reunification with the deceased after death. For some Jewish clients that I have worked with, this made the acceptance of the death more difficult.

Some cultures have a completely different view of death. Asian Indians who follow the Hindu faith believe in reincarnation. According to the Hindu culture, life has no beginning or end, only an eternal web. Hindus believe that life begins before birth and continues after death. Life on this earth is viewed as merely a passage in time toward a destiny (Karma) that we have no power to alter. From the time of death the soul leaves the body and enters another being to continue its evolution of its Karma, until it finally evolves, often through multiple reincarnations of the person through cycles of birth, life, and death, to a final passage into nirvana.[5] In this belief system, death is not something to be feared but celebrated as another step toward the person reaching Karma. Obviously, this belief system greatly impacts the mourning process of the survivors since death has a very different meaning than in Western culture. Death is not final or permanent, but rather a step closer to one's final destination.

It is critical for mental health practitioners who are counseling the newly bereaved to know about a particular culture's belief system and mourning rituals regarding death. Monica McGoldrick suggests asking the following questions:

- What are the prescribed rituals for caring for the dying and the dead body, for disposal of the body, and to commemorate the loss?
- What are the religious group's beliefs about what happens after death?
- What do they believe about appropriate emotional expression and memorializing of the lost person?
- What are the gender rules for handling the death?
- Are certain deaths particularly stigmatized (e.g. suicide) or traumatic for the group? And if so, are there culturally sanctioned customs for helping families move beyond the sense of stigma?[6]

The question about gender is particularly important in many cultures. Men and women are assigned specific roles and must abide by specific rules. In our society, men and women are raised very differently. In his bestseller, Men Are from Mars, Women are from Venus, John Gray points out how women are process-oriented and men are solution-oriented. This is seen quite clearly in bereavement where women generally take on the social and emotional tasks of grief, including caretaking of the terminally ill, the expression of grief and attending to the needs of the survivors; whereas men focus on the practical tasks such as funeral arrangements, selecting the coffin, paying fees, and other "administrative tasks".

Kenneth Doka has developed the term "masculine grief" to describe how many men deal with their grief. Masculine grievers seem more comfortable in dealing with grief cognitively and actively. Hence, they may immerse themselves in activity. They choose legal or physical actions in response to the loss. For example, Jim whose son was lost and assumed dead after his training plane crashed, found solace by being actively involved in the search. Other masculine grievers take an active role in funeral planning. All of those are typical of masculine grief.[7] Furthermore, men are socialized to be self-sufficient and see themselves as protectors, providers, and problem solvers. Consequently, it is very difficult for them to reach out for help. With their cognitive emphasis, they do not see the value of discussing a loss. This was very evident with a male student I had in a support group with several female students. While the girls spoke very openly about how the loss of a parent had changed their lives, the young man's usual comment was, "Why talk about it? It will not change anything". This is reflective of a realistic or practical orientation that many men have. Unless a problem can be fixed, it is not worth thinking about. Obviously, grief has no easy fix which explains why so few men seek bereavement counseling or support groups. Women on the other hand are not looking for a quick fix when they seek help. They are more apt to pursue counseling to lessen their pain and gain a better understanding of their grief. For mental health practitioners in a school setting, these very significant gender differences in grieving need to be respected when facilitating a support group. If the facilitator emphasizes too much of a feminine grieving style, she may lose the boys in the group.

In conclusion, the nature of grief is very complex with psychological, cultural, and even biological factors at work. This explains the very individual way that people experience grief. No two people grieve exactly the same way. Grief can be best described as an emotional wound and has parallels to physical wounds or injuries. There is a long healing process, with advances and setbacks that often feel like a roller coaster ride. As with a serious physical injury, the individual may feel progress for a few days then relapse into a more painful period. As the good days begin to outnumber the bad, healing is accelerated. While healing will reach a point where the person feels whole again, as with a serious physical injury, the individual is never quite the same gain. Like someone with an old injury who feels sore on a frigid day, the mourner bears an emotional scar that can be reactivated during special sentimental moments when those feelings of grief resurface.

UNRESOLVED GRIEF

As noted in the previous chapter, grief is a very individual experience. Our unique psychological make-up and cultural influences form a mosaic which determines our very individual grief reaction. This can especially be seen in the duration of grief. One of the most commonly asked questions by the newly bereaved is: How long will my grief last? Many societies have tried to designate a time period by which grief is completed. In our society, the one year anniversary is often used as the end point. I have worked with hundreds of newly bereaved persons and I have seen some whose grieving period may have been a few months while for others it has taken several years. Therefore, just as there is no standard or correct way to grieve, there is no time frame that fits all. However, there are factors which impede or stifle the healing process that caregivers and mental health practitioners must be aware of in working with the newly bereaved.

When someone dies, there are always unresolved issues. Some may be very profound such as not having said goodbye in cases of sudden death. Others may deal with concerns regarding the medical care received which can lead to investigations and even lawsuits. Still other unresolved issues may deal with the more mundane such as financial matters and what to do with the personal belongings of the deceased. These are all often referred to as unfinished business. In most cases these are successfully addressed by the newly bereaved with time, patience, and the support of family and friends. However, some unresolved issues present challenges that are overwhelming and become a hindrance to the healing process. In almost every model of grief, acceptance of the death is a key task or phase/stage that must addressed for healing to take place. In cases where the circumstances of the death have left many unanswered questions or mystery surrounds the death, acceptance of the death becomes very difficult. The most obvious examples are where the body cannot be found such as in MIAs from wars, plane crashes, natural destruction (earthquakes, tsunamis), and terrorist attacks such as 9/11 where bodies were incinerated, leaving no remains. In such cases, the loved ones of the deceased often hold on to a very small possibility that somehow the person survived the tragic event and is still alive somewhere. Without the body, incomplete acceptance and lack of closure can cause some to become stuck in their grief. Similarly, where the body is found but there are many questions as to the cause of death, acceptance can also be stymied. A good example of this is in cases of suicide or homicide. The survivors are usually left with so many questions about the death and why they could not prevent it. The guilt, blame, anger and sense of rejection they experience are overwhelming, and it may take years for the survivors to work through their grief. In cases where the murder or suicide is witnessed, the survivors will be traumatized and may relive the event through flashbacks for years.

Tragic accidents may have the same effects, especially when there is a great deal of mystery surrounding the death. I experienced an extreme example of this as a school counselor in a suburban high school. A group of seniors decided to go to a Caribbean Island on spring break. During one evening they took a "booze cruise" and boarded an overcrowded party boat where there was drinking, eating, dancing, and very little supervision. One student from the group fell or jumped into the water and was killed by the propeller of the boat. When the crew of the boat realized what happened, they returned to port. There was no proper investigation of how the youngster wound up in the water. The island was not under the legal jurisdiction of the U.S. Over two hundred predominantly high school students were on the boat and all but a few were released without being questioned. Furthermore, his friends claimed that they did not know how he wound up in the water and refused to speak about the incident. The devastated parents conducted their own investigation, first for his body which was never found. Then, they investigated why their son was overboard at the time of his death. They hired private investigators who tracked down many of the students on the boat and spent months trying to determine what happened that night. While the investigation led to several theories, one of which was that a friend dared the victim to jump into the water as part of a bet, there was no conclusive evidence to explain what happened. His parents may still be haunted by some of those unanswered questions and their grief is ongoing.

Another type of unresolved grief is the relationship that the loved one had with deceased. Generally speaking, the stronger the emotional bonds with the deceased, the more intense the grief. When those bonds become an integral part of the functioning and well-being of the survivor, an overly-dependent relationship with the deceased may exist and can become a detriment to the mourner. I have seen many examples of this where a spouse took care of a very ill mate for many years. The survivor's caregiver role became so central to his existence that when the death occurs, he experiences a loss of purpose and even identity. The grief process becomes even more formidable as rebuilding a sense of purpose and identity becomes part of the grief work.

Adolescents who lose a parent face a threat to their identity formation. Our parents are our advocates, caregivers, and role models. The mentoring teenagers receive from their parents help guide them to become responsible and independent adults. Parental loss often leads adolescents to suppress their grief since they have very little experience with death, and they fear that their grief will overwhelm them. Consequently, some teenagers experience a delayed grief reaction which may resurface many years later.

Conflicted relationships where there is much ambivalence can also impact the grief process. Two people may love one another but because of their different views or personality differences, they are always at odds with one another. They care about each other but just cannot seem to make the relationship work. When one of them dies, the survivor experiences an additional loss, that is, the opportunity to make this valued relationship right again. This lost opportunity leaves the survivor with a powerful feeling of regret that the relationship ended with unresolved conflicts. This is quite common with teenagers who often have a very contentious relationship with one or both parents as they strive for independence and adulthood.

Another factor that can influence the healing process is the mental health of the griever. Individuals who have a history of psychological problems, such as depression, low self-esteem, anxiety disorders, or those who are socially withdrawn, are psychologically fragile. They are going to struggle more with an important loss because they lack the strength to deal with the emotional and psychological challenges presented by grief. Furthermore, individuals with prior unresolved losses may find a new loss overwhelming since the old losses tend to resurface with each new loss. Consequently, flashbacks and painful memories are triggered by the new loss and suddenly the person is grieving new and old losses simultaneously. This can often be seen in adults who suppressed the loss of a family member in their childhood or teenage years. The death of a neighbor or distant relative many years later may trigger an unusually intense grief reaction because the original loss resurfaces and is finally being experienced.

Unresolved grief does not need to be permanent. Most individuals can, with time, grief work, and possibly therapy, work through these obstacles to healing. However, mental health practitioners in school settings and elsewhere need to be aware when individuals are stuck in their grief. One of the first things to look for is a lack of progression. Time is an important component in the healing process provided the individual is actively engaged in grief work. Therefore, we can expect a progression in the healing process. The newly bereaved's thoughts, feelings, and physical reactions will change after many months of grief work. A conversation with a person who suffered a loss a few months ago should be very different than a follow-up conversation with that person two years later. In the original conversation, one would expect very intense emotions, and much of the conversation would resemble an autopsy. In other words, there is often an obsession with discussing the details of the death and the events that led up to it. The follow-up conversation two years later should be very different. While some emotions may be evident, the emotional intensity should be much less. Furthermore, while there may be some discussion of the death and past events, the predominant conversation one would expect would be about "picking up the pieces".

The focus of that conversation should be the present and future, and what adjustments the person has made in living a life without the deceased. If the follow-up conversation sounds almost identical to the original conversation, this is an indicator that the person is stuck in their grief. If there is no improvement in symptoms over a significant time period, one can surmise that there is unresolved grief. The literature on bereavement also refers to it as "complicated grief". This was very evident to me during a phone conversation I had with a woman who was very distraught and spoke in excruciating detail of her husband's illness and eventual death. I learned after the conversation that he died five years ago. As it turned out, her unresolved grief was caused by her own bout with cancer. In trying to preserve her life, she suppressed her grief for her husband. I have also witnessed this with teenagers. While speaking with me, a student who lost her mother 9 years ago became very teary-eyed and was not able to continue with the conversation about her interest in joining a support group. I later learned that her father had remarried after his wife's death and she felt inhibited about discussing her mother in the new blended family.

Another indicator of unresolved grief is chronic depression. While almost all newly bereaved experience depression, it tends to be episodic in nature. An individual may experience several days of depression and then, sometimes inexplicably, it lifts for a few days. This is part of the roller coaster phenomenon most people experience with grief. Even suicidal thoughts can occur, provided that they are fleeting. For example, a person may wish not to wake up in the morning, but by the next day the thought passes and there is no specific planning to take one's life. In chronic depression, it is constant and always there. The suicidal thoughts have specificity and planning is evident.

Another sign would be the person's level of functioning. It has always amazed me how the newly bereaved manage to function even while experiencing overwhelming grief. They go to work, provide for their families, take care of their homes, and attend social functions. Even though their zest for living is gone and they are just going through the motions of living, they are able to do what is necessary. Those who withdraw socially and are not able to function at work or home may be experiencing unresolved grief. This also includes individuals who turn to alcohol or drugs to self-medicate. For teenagers, this may be manifested by failing grades, poor attendance, quitting previous clubs or sports teams, rebelling against authority figures, and/or turning to substance abuse to escape from the painful reality.

As mentioned earlier, one's personal history could by itself be a warning sign of unresolved grief. Those who have experienced psychological difficulties or a prior history of loss through death, divorce, injury, a disability, or abandonment can be very vulnerable. These individuals are ill-equipped to deal with the loss of a loved one.

The more of these signs (no improvement in symptoms over time, chronic depression, poor level of functioning, and difficult past history) that are present in an individual, the greater the likelihood that the person is stuck in unresolved grief and will require therapeutic intervention.

HOW ADOLESCENTS EXPERIENCE GRIEF

Adolescents face the same challenges as adults in terms of the stages, phases and tasks of grief. However, there are differences in the way they experience grief. Unlike adults, grief is not constant, but more intermittent and episodic. Periods of intense grief can be followed by periods where grief appears almost non-existent. They often do this through play, which provides a break from grief. Play serves as a distraction and helps reestablish a sense of normalcy in their lives. In a training program that I facilitated for those who work with the newly bereaved, a funeral director in the class had a very unique way of describing this phenomenon. He observed that children and adolescents in his funeral home can display the same somber and serious demeanor as adults when in the viewing room during a wake. Yet, in a matter of minutes, when they are outside and socializing with their friends, they become happy and playful. He termed this ability to quickly turn grief on and off as "jump grieving". To help them, he set a room aside in the funeral home where children and adolescence can go for play, fun and relief. This is actually a healthy defense mechanism since they do not have the life experience and maturity to manage the emotional and psychological turmoil of grief. They seem to be able to shut it off so that they are not consumed by grief as adults often are.

Another difference in the way they experience grief is that in adolescence, the self-conscious teenager does not want to stand out or appear different from his peers. Grief brings a tremendous amount of unwanted attention from adults in their lives as teachers, relatives, or friends of the family seek them out to offer sympathy and support. Many students have described to me the awkwardness they felt the first day that they returned to school. While socializing with friends, well-meaning staff members would pull them aside to offer sympathy. Then, they would have to explain the death to those who did not know what happened. Consequently, many adolescents try to keep the information private and are even secretive to avoid the excessive attention. This makes grieving more difficult for them, because they are eliminating social supports that can be very helpful in dealing with grief.

Additionally, from an adolescent's perspective, death is something that is affiliated with old age. Although intellectually they know that death can happen to anyone regardless of age, in their world it is very distant and removed. Therefore, when a peer is killed in a car crash or a young family member dies suddenly, it can provide a jolt to their reality. It makes them confront their own mortality; their cockiness and bravado are often replaced with insecurity. I have witnessed this in schools where the toughest male who is fearless on the athletic field totally crumbles with the death of a classmate. At such times, teenagers really bond with one another. They would rather be with each other than with school mental health professionals, teachers, or other adults in their lives. Furthermore, the insecurity brought on by an ill-timed death may cause some regression. I remember the reaction of one of the friends of the student who was killed on the booze cruise. His mother called me with great concern, because her son was afraid to sleep in his own room and insisted on sleeping on the floor next to her bed. This went on for a few weeks as he tried to come to terms with the vulnerability and loss of security he felt that was brought on by his friend's death.

Perhaps the most fundamental loss that a teenager can experience is the death of a parent. Where else in their world of self-discovery and learning by trial and error can they receive unconditional love? Mistakes they make with peers, teachers, employers can cost them dearly, but mistakes they make with parents carry much less risk. They know that their parents will forgive them, give them another chance, and most importantly, continue to love them. Therefore, this sense of security in the unconditional love of their parents often causes teenagers to indulge in risky behavior, such as testing curfews and experimenting with substances and sex, as they strive for separation, independence, and their own identity. Consequently, for most teenagers and their parents, this is a period of frequent conflict. Vicious things are said in the heat of an argument. While teenagers have unfinished business with the death of a loved one as adults would, if a parent dies during this tumultuous period, they often experience a sense of responsibility. This is especially evident if the death is perceived as stress related. I had a student in a support group whose mother died of a burst aneurism. She blamed herself and was convinced that her frequent fights with her mother were a prime contributing factor to her death. For most adults, it is easier to put things into proper perspective. It is easier to rationalize that conflicts with adolescents are a normal part of living and that the person died of an illness, not a conflict. Having wished a parent dead at the height of a verbal altercation did not cause it to come true. However, lacking life experience, adolescents often have difficulty seeing the larger picture, and blame themselves for the death. Additionally, the loss of a parent eliminates the one person that can give them unconditional love at a time that they need it most. It is a tremendous blow to their self-esteem, and can have an impact on their development into confident, self-assured adults.

Another important characteristic of adolescent grief is in the nature of their loss. When a loved one dies, there are many losses in addition to losing the person. For an adult, other losses may include companionship, a sense of security, financial stability, intimacy, identity, and perhaps most of all a feeling that part of you is missing. It has been said that when you lose a parent or sibling, you lose your past, when you lose a spouse or life partner, you lose your present; and when you lose a child, you lose your future. I am not sure of the origin of this view of loss, but it carries great wisdom. In my personal experience, as well as professional experience in working with adults, it certainly has been a valid model. I have discussed this concept in my adolescent support groups to better understand the nature of their loss. In their perspective, they have lost all three: past, present and future. They have lived their entire lives with their parents so they certainly lose part of their past. In their present life, they live with their parents and are very dependent on their mentoring, guidance, and support so they clearly lose part of their present. The one that resonates most with many teenagers is the loss of their future. In the adolescent support groups that I have facilitated, they frequently voice concerns about not having the deceased parent at their games, school functions, graduation, move-in day at college, and at their wedding. Girls who have lost their father worry about who will give them away at their wedding. They also worry about the surviving parent. If something happens to the surviving parent, who will take care of them? If one parent dies, surely the same can happen to the other parent. They can become an orphan. They live with this pervasive sense of anxiety about their future and it becomes part of their grief experience.

Some important studies have been conducted which gives valuable empirical evidence of how adolescents are affected by the death of a parent or sibling. Phyllis Silverman and J. William Worden conducted a study of children who lost a parent which revealed some very significant findings on the natural course of bereavement in children 6-17 years of age. In the Harvard Child Bereavement Study, they did a longitudinal study of 125 school age children from 70 families and followed them for two years. They used a control group of non-bereaved children with matching factors such as age, gender, grade, religion and community. The children, surviving parents and family received assessments to determine the bereavement journey of these children. Below is a summary of their findings.

The study revealed that most children (80%) fared well at the first and second anniversaries of the death. The 20% that were not coping well exceeded the percentage in the control group that were not doing well during that period. The differences between the control group and bereaved children not doing well actually increased between the first and second years, which gives support to there being a late effect of loss on these children.

Children doing well came from cohesive families where there was open communication about the deceased and where they experienced fewer life changes and disruptions in normal routine. Families who coped actively rather than passively and who could find something positive in a difficult situation had children who made a better adaption to the loss.

Children not doing well tended to come from families experiencing a large number of stressors and changes as a result of the death and having a surviving parent who was young, depressed and not coping well. These children showed lower self-esteem and less ability to control what had happened to them in life.

The most powerful predictor of how a child adjusts to the death of the parent is the level of functioning of the surviving parent. In cases where the parent is not functioning well, these children showed more anxiety, depression, as well as sleep and health problems.

The loss of a mother, in general, had a greater negative impact than the loss of a father. For most families, the death of a mother brings about more life changes in the family and in most cases, the mother is the emotional caretaker of the family. Her central role in the family has a greater impact on the bereaved children, especially by the second year of the loss. Mother loss was associated with more maladaptive behaviors such as the children exhibiting emotional/behavior problems including acting out, high levels of anxiety, lower self-esteem and a weaker belief in one's own self-efficacy.

Most children who were given the choice decided to participate in the funeral. Better outcomes were evident in children who received some preparation before the service. The ability to recapture memories of the funeral and talk about it increased over time. Including children in the planning of the funeral had a positive effect, helping them feel important and useful at a time when many are feeling overwhelmed.

Many children remained connected to their dead parent through talking to them, thinking about them, dreaming about them, and locating them in a specific place. Children with strong continuing bonds to the deceased parent seemed better able to show their emotional pain, to talk to others about the death, and to accept support from families and friends.

Bereaved teenagers feel different from their peers because of the loss. Furthermore, they feel misunderstood by their friends who have not experienced the loss of a parent. The subgroup that seems to be especially affected by this is girls who lost their mother and are left with a father. Another finding deals with parental dating in the first year of bereavement. The researchers found that these children exhibited withdrawn behavior, acting out behavior and somatic symptoms, especially if the parent was a father. Conversely, if there was a suitable time period, engagement and remarriage actually had a healthy effect on the children. They were less apt to be anxious, depressed and less worried about the safety of the surviving parent.

Three things that children need after the death of a parent are support, nurturance and continuity. Continued routine activity is very important, especially with such things as mealtimes, bedtime, homework assignments and after school activities. Providing these may be difficult for a surviving parent, and particularly difficult for a surviving father. Childhood grief is best facilitated in the presence of a consistent adult who is able to meet the child's needs and help the child express feelings about loss.[8]

The researchers concluded that bereaved children have specific needs that counselors need to address in order to help them. They need to know that they will be cared for. "Who will take care of me?" is a question on the minds of most children. If something happens to the surviving parent, they need reassurance that someone will be there to take care of them. Furthermore, bereaved children need to know that they did not cause the death out of their anger or shortcomings. They need clear information about the death; they need to feel important and involved with such things as the funeral and memorial services. They also need routine activity; they need someone who will listen to their questions; and bereaved children need ways to remember the dead person. Adults can assist with this last need by starting a memory book where the youngster can put pictures, stories, and other items memorializing the parent and the special times that shared together. As they grow older, they will revisit the scrapbook and it becomes a way of keeping the memory of the person alive.

***

A similar study was done on adolescent sibling grief. With the help of Compassionate Friends, an international support group of bereaved parents and siblings of deceased children, 230 families were invited to participate in the study. The researchers developed a questionnaire which was distributed to the family. A total of 157 adolescents from these families returned completed questionnaires. The respondents were 13 to 18 years of age and had lost a sibling within the last five years.

The results revealed that for these youngsters their bereavement did not proceed in stages or phases, nor was there a growing detachment from the deceased sibling with the passage of time. Instead they found that the bereaved siblings maintained a persistent and ongoing attachment to the deceased sibling that was not time bound. Comments from the questionnaires indicated that the attachment spanned past dimensions (i.e. regrets over silly arguments, why it happened), present dimensions (watch over me,

How is it in heaven?) and future dimensions (I will see you later, I will be spending eternity with you). In the sibling adolescent bereavement process reflected in this study, the bereaved siblings learned to live with the physical absence of the deceased sibling while simultaneously maintaining the emotional presence of the dead brother or sister.[9] A student in one of my support groups perhaps describes this attachment best. While she accepted the death of her brother, she maintained an emotional bond or relationship with him through pictures, personal belongings, dreams, memories, and a strong faith that she will see him again one day in an afterlife.

A related study, using the same 157 subjects and their responses on the questionnaire, sought to find factors that help or hinder in adolescent sibling grief. Hogan found that 69% of the students indicated that family members were of assistance, especially their mothers and fathers. Their parents provided support and comfort by helping them accept the normality of their feelings and by sharing memories of the deceased sibling with them. Additionally, 31% of these youngsters reported that other kin besides their parents (grandparents, aunts, other siblings) were helpful to them. In these cases the death of the child brought the families together in dealing with the aftermath of loss, and the family was seen as a support network for the bereaved adolescent. Many of the bereaved adolescents (51%) found help in friends who were there when they needed them. Other factors that were helpful included being engaged in stress reducing activities (17%) such as writing, playing a musical instrument and keeping very busy, and having a personal belief system or inner strength (12%).

In terms of what hindered adolescent sibling grief, the personal coping system of the youngster was compromised by reoccurring intrusive, uninvited, painful thoughts that usually dealt with the circumstances and events surrounding the death. Hogan reported that 36% of the respondents expressed varying degrees of guilt, shame or blame for their perceived inability to assist their dying sibling or prevent their death. The majority of these responses were given by siblings whose brothers or sisters died of unexpected traumatic causes such as suicide, homicide or an accident. Other respondents (40%) experienced a prevailing sense of loneliness following the death. The deceased sibling was considered a best friend who was missed terribly. This finding was especially evident where the bereaved sibling was now an only child. Families that hindered grieving siblings tended to be those where there were conflicts and family discord. Family members blaming each other for their shortcomings made the grieving adolescent feel upset and angry (15%). Furthermore, 26% reported that seeing their parents distressed over the loss of a child was an additional burden for them to bear. Some of these respondents reported distress that their parents were emotionally unavailable due to their preoccupation with the deceased child. Finally, 15% of the respondents expressed disappointment in a social system that they perceived as insensitive. The behavior of these unidentified individuals was characterized as being judgmental and they gave unsolicited advice on how the youngster should grieve. They made insensitive remarks, "I know how you feel" and "You should be over it by now". These comments and advice were viewed by the bereaved adolescent as pretentious, presumptuous, and preventing them from dealing with the death on their own terms.[10]

Aside from being insensitive and judgmental, these remarks shut off any communication. How is the youngster supposed to respond to such closed statements? The best response would be one that allows a youngster the opportunity to express his own individual grief through an open statement or question such as, "How are you coping?" or "What are your favorite memories of John?" Such responses allow the sibling the freedom to take the conversation in whatever direction he chooses.

HOW DEATH IMPACTS THE FAMILY

As the reader can see from Worden's study, the family has a huge impact on the adolescent's adjustment to the death of a parent. It can provide the necessary support, structure and nurturance to make a smooth adjustment, or it can undermine the youngster by not addressing these needs effectively. In the literature on family systems theory, we learn that each family has a hierarchical structure with parents at the top of the pyramid and the children below them. There are boundaries that separate parents and children, and each member of the family has defined roles. The boundaries in a well-functioning family have some flexibility so that children can express concerns and provide input, but ultimately the parents are the decision makers. The family seeks to maintain equilibrium, so that in crisis situations there are mechanisms to restore order. For instance, if the parents are having difficulties and the marriage seems in jeopardy, often one of the children will exhibit disruptive behavior at school or home. This draws attention away from the marital problems and onto the children, keeping the parents together and the family intact. The death of a family member puts the family in crisis. Other members of the family will try to restore equilibrium by assuming the roles that were performed by the deceased. If the family member was a parent, the structure of the family has been altered. Someone now needs to assume the roles played by the deceased parent. If the surviving parent is a strong person, she will assume these roles as best as possible. However, in many families, the adolescent child will assume those roles and becomes the surrogate parent. This places an unfair burden on the adolescent and gives him adult-like responsibilities. This can have negative consequences as the structure of the family and its equilibrium has been compromised. In support groups I facilitated in schools, I met such adolescent surrogate parents, and most have been resentful of being put in this situation. One particular student I worked with was a young lady whose mother died of cancer. She was a high school senior who lived with her father and a brother in elementary school. Her mother died when she was in the eighth grade and her brother was four years old at the time. Her father was a rabbi who spent long hours serving his congregation and community. He stuck with these traditional roles and did not expand his parenting role. Consequently, the 8th grader started to become a mother figure to the four year old. She would come immediately home after school to watch her brother and throughout high school continued in this role of surrogate mother with great resentment. She was applying to colleges far away from home so she could escape this role that robbed her of a social life and involvement in school activities.

If a child dies in the family, again the structure and equilibrium of the family is put in peril. The child played a role in the family and now some of the siblings may assume the role. If that child helped to keep the family together by getting in trouble and redirecting the parent's attention, one of the siblings may now assume that role. Often the parents are so consumed by their grief over the lost child that they unintentionally ignore the needs of the remaining children. The children often interpret this as meaning that the deceased child was the favorite of the parents. Again, the balance and equilibrium of the family is compromised because in the eyes of the surviving children, the deceased child is in a higher position than they are.

This was brilliantly illustrated in the movie Ordinary People. In this movie two brothers were in a boating accident and only one survived. The one who died was the high achieving child who made the parents proud and the survivor was an underachiever who did not live up to their expectations. Throughout the movie, the message that the surviving son received from the parents was that they wished he had died instead of his brother. Equally problematic for the family is when the parents have a new baby which becomes the replacement for the one who died. The replacement child carries all the hopes and dreams that the parents had for the deceased child and occupies a higher position in the family hierarchy. This will leave a very unbalanced family ripe for strife.

In addition to disharmony caused by families with weak structure and equilibrium, poor communication and family secrets can also undermine the family. In my work as a bereavement counselor, I have seen how the death of a family member can pull a family together or apart. Families that have good communication, where information is shared openly and honestly, and where children's feelings and opinions are respected and included in important family decisions, usually rally and pull together when a family member dies. Families where there is weak structure and/ or poor communication, and where children are not included in important family matters, often breed unhealthy levels of distrust, resentment and misunderstanding. Family secrets develop and when the children do not have correct information, they provide their own explanations which lead to myths. When a family member dies in such a family, it pulls apart, because the surviving family members do not have the relationship and cohesiveness to help each another. If secrets are discovered after the death, a sense of betrayal can similarly undermine family unity. Members from such estranged families tend to suffer in silence and isolation.

In families where the parents are divorced, grief becomes more complicated because it may cause old unresolved conflicts to resurface. Grief becomes another venue where blame, bitterness and retribution are relived. In such cases, grieving the divorce may need to take place before grieving the individual.

Some of the characteristics mentioned above in poorly functioning families are well illustrated in a family which I counseled several years ago. I received a call from the mother of a 15 year old female high school freshman. She called me because the school was very worried about her daughter and they felt she needed counseling. She went on to explain that her husband had died six months ago and her daughter was taking it very hard. The presenting problem was that the student was being very disruptive in school. She would have emotional outbursts in class, run to the nurse's office and stay there for extended periods of time. Furthermore, the school counselor noted that she had stopped associating with her old friends and started hanging out with a new group of friends who might be a bad influence on her. The mother made it clear that she was acting on the school's recommendation, and did not share the same level of concern. She just felt that the daughter was just having a tough time because of her father's death. I agreed to see the daughter and obtained the mother's permission to follow up with the school.

At our first counseling session, GL impressed me as a very thoughtful and expressive teenager who spoke very candidly about her father's illness and death. She shared with me a poem that she wrote about her father that was very powerful. In the poem, she revealed her father's playful and loving nature, and the wonderful relationship they had. It also reflected her struggle to understand this terrible tragedy and to come to terms with the reality of his death. She clearly missed him and could not understand why a good person had to die while criminals go on living. After I read it, we discussed the poem and it was clear to me that GL was much closer to her father than mother. It appeared to me that he was the emotional caretaker of the family, which is the role usually taken by the mother.

At our next counseling session, we discussed some of the concerns expressed by the school. When I questioned her on the emotional outbursts, GL said that this usually happens when a class is very boring. Her attention begins to drift and she starts daydreaming about her father. She becomes very upset and the teacher does not know what to do with her so GL asks to be sent to go the nurse's office. The nurse who has a good relationship with GL, would allow her to talk which calms her down and eventually she would return to class. GL disagreed with the school on her sudden change of friends. She found it easier sometimes to hang out with peers who did not know her or her family well. With her close friends, who knew her family for many years, she sometimes felt awkward since they really did not know what to say to her. GL just saw this as a temporary accommodation until she and her friends could act normal again. For the remainder of the session, she talked about her father and reminisced about all the great things they did together. I followed up with the school the next day. I spoke to the nurse who sounded like a very kind and compassionate person. She had a special relationship with GL, who saw her as someone she could trust and confide in. The nurse was the only person in the school that GL would seek out when she became upset and wanted to talk about her father.

I also spoke to the school counselor, who confirmed many of the things that both GL and the school nurse reported. I wanted to see how GL and her mother interacted, so for the third session, I met with both of them. The session began uneventfully, with GL reviewing her week at school and the mother joining in at appropriate moments to elaborate or clarify on what GL said. Then GL began talking about her father, and her mother started to cry. GL became very agitated. She said, "there you go again", and stopped talking.

There was an awkward silence that followed. Then the mother explained that while discussing her husband was upsetting to her, her children certainly had her permission to talk about him. At that point, I separated the two and continued the session with GL alone. She was very angry and reported that when she or one of her three older brothers mentioned her father, the mother would cry and the discussion would end. Consequently, a conspiracy of silence had developed in the family. None of the children would bring up the father in conversation because it would upset the mother. It became an unwritten taboo to mention the father at home. GL hated this and resented her mother for it, but followed along with her brothers. It was also curious to me, because the mother was in a support group that I facilitated for newly widowed individuals, and did not cry when discussing her husband. I began to realize that GL was grieving at school because she could not grieve at home. Her emotional outbursts were a reaction to the grief she was suppressing at home. The school nurse had become her emotional caretaker who she could turn to when she needed to talk about her father. After five counseling sessions, it was clear to me that GL's grief for her father was very genuine and normal, but her grief was being stifled at home by very unhealthy family dynamics. The lack of communication in the family was pulling it apart, and each member was grieving alone and in isolation. I shared my observations with the mother. She disagreed and insisted that the children could talk about their father at any time. I recommended that the next counseling session be with the entire family: GL, her mother and three brothers. My feeling was that if this conspiracy of silence could be addressed, it would benefit the children. The mother said she would think about it but never called again for an appointment. I surmised that the conspiracy of silence, which would have surfaced and been challenged in a family counseling session, was too great a threat for her, which prompted her to end counseling. I did see the mother several months later at a reunion of her support group. She said that GL was doing better, but the mother was actually worse than when she was in the group. GL found ways to grieve for her father outside of home, which enabled her to heal, while the mother seemed stuck in her own grief.

ASSISTING THE NEWLY BEREAVED STUDENT

Many schools lack a coherent and consistent policy for preparing the newly bereaved student's return to school. Unfortunately, many parents do not even inform the school until the student is already back. It should be noted in the student handbook and in orientation meetings with the parents that when the student is absent due to a death in the family, the school should be contacted as soon as possible. This information should be relayed to the child study team which usually consists of the school counselor, school nurse, administrator, psychologist, and a teacher. When the team receives this information, they should convene the same day and develop a game plan for the student's return to school. Someone on the team should contact the parent and discuss the needs of the student. The game plan should consist of several key elements. The first is who should know about the student's loss? Most students I have worked with felt that the death of a family member is a private matter, and only those working directly with the student should be informed. This would include the student's teachers, coach, dean, and anyone else in direct contact with the student. A second element would be assigning a staff member who would monitor the student when he returns to school. This should be the school counselor, unless there is someone else on the team who has a much stronger relationship with the student. This person would meet briefly with the student, initially every day and later weekly, to assist with his transition back to school. There should be only one person making regular contact with the student. Students have reported to me how upsetting it can be when several well-meaning staff members are asking students the same questions and expressing the same concerns.

A third important component of the game plan would be making any needed adjustments to the student's academic responsibilities, such making up tests and completing assignments or projects that are due. Again, this needs to be discussed with the parent, student, and affected teachers.

In most cases, students are given extended time to meet these academic responsibilities; and in some cases, where appropriate, the student can be excused from an assignment or test. As reported in Worden's study, it is important for the bereaved student to have structure and routine so adjustments should be limited. Upon return to school, the counselor would meet with the student and review the game plan. The counselor would also be in communication with the teachers who would alert the counselor if anything of concern should arise. If, at the daily meetings with the school counselor, the student indicates he has needs not being met, the counselor would relay this information back to the child study team. They can then modify the game plan.

The information regarding the student's loss should be saved and noted on the student's records. When the student transitions to a new school, grade, or even a new semester where there is a change of teachers and counselor, the new staff should be notified of the loss. I have dealt with angry teachers who made a reference to a student's parents in class, i.e. "I am going to call your mother if you do not do your homework", only to find out that the mother is deceased. These teachers can easily develop a dislike for pupil personnel support staff (counselors, social workers, psychologists) when they feel embarrassed in front of their class for not knowing such important background information.

The game plan should be flexible and take the student's wishes into consideration. For instance, if the student is showing resistance to meeting with the counselor regularly, these meetings can take place only on an as-needed basis. As long as the counselor is in communication with the teachers, the student's progress can be monitored. Forcing counseling sessions on a student, even if well-meaning, can be counterproductive. One student whose father was a police officer who died in 9/11, reported to me that every year afterwards on that day she would be seen by a member of the pupil personnel staff for a counseling session. This practice continued through her elementary, middle school, and now high school years. She dreaded that day not only for the tragic memories it brought back but also for the mandatory counseling session she would have to endure. The pupil personnel staff should have elicited feedback from the student on the value of the counseling session. If the student indicated that the practice was not helpful, then it should have not continued. Perhaps just alerting the teachers and others who are in regular contact with the student should have sufficed.

Sometimes a family member dies when the student is in school which brings up the question of what is the school's role in such a situation. With all the electronic devices we have today, it is possible that other students can find out about the death before the student knows. One student reported to me that when she was in middle school an administrator pulled her out of class and told her he had very important information to share with her. He wanted to do it privately so she would have to come to his office. She experienced a very high level of anxiety on the way to his office suspecting that something very bad had happened. Once she arrived in his office, he told her that her father had died. To receive such news from a person she hardly knew made the loss even more devastating. The well-meaning administrator wanted to tell her because other students became aware of this news, and it was spreading around the school. He wanted to tell her before she heard it from other students.

Devastating news such as the death of a loved one will be always remembered by the survivor. It becomes a traumatic moment in our lives, becoming etched in our memory and relived many times as we grieve for the loss. Should such tragic news be given by a relative stranger?

I think a better approach may have been to ask the teacher to send the student to his office with a note. Once the student arrived, the administrator could have simply asked the student to remain in his office because a parent was going to pick her up. If the student asks why, the administrator could simply say she was needed at home for a personal matter. When the parent or relative picks up the student, the student should be escorted out of school and the news should be given in the car or at home. The news should not be given in school, because the upset student may encounter peers while leaving school and no teenager wants to be on public display at such a sensitive time. Obviously, the student is probably going to suspect bad news in this approach as well, but at least the news will be delivered privately by someone the student knows and loves. Therefore, that traumatic moment that is forever etched in the student's memory will be with a family member and not a stranger.

As noted earlier in the book, adults are often mystified by an adolescent's reaction to grief. If they do not see visible signs of grief, they begin to worry. They expect the teenager to cry and become overwhelmed with sadness as adults do. As we have learned, many teenagers may carry on with their lives with little outward signs of grief. The typical parent may interpret this to mean that something has gone wrong and that the student is in need of counseling. I have received many such calls where a very anxious parent calls the school looking for counseling for their child. In such instances, I have interviewed the student and explained that some of the adults in his life were worried about him. The purpose of the interview is always to try to assess the student's level of functioning. When speaking to the student, I always begin by expressing my condolences and the reason for the interview. Here are some of the questions I would ask.

- Why do you think that adults in your life are worried about you?
- What are they seeing that has them worried?
- How are you coping with your loss?
- What work did you miss when you were out of school?
- What progress have you made with completing this work?
- How have your friends responded to you since your father died?
- In what ways have your friends been supportive?
- What other things can they do to support you?
- To what extent are you still involved in school activities?
- What are your interests outside of school? Are you still pursuing these interests?
- How has your loss affected your relationship with the adults in the school?
- How has the death impacted your family?
- How has the loss affected your relationship with other members of your family?

The questions focus on academic functioning, social functioning, level of engagement in school activities and outside interests, behavior in school, and family life. If the student is not communicative or appears uncomfortable, I would end the interview before its completion and report to the parent that the student is not ready to discuss the loss. For students who are verbal and appear comfortable with the interview, I would try to determine the student's level of functioning in those areas mentioned. If the student seems to be functioning well in these areas, or at least functioning at the about the same level as before the loss, I would call the parent back and report my findings. I would stress that teenagers grieve differently than most adults and as long as the teenager knows that help is available, the parent should just let the teenager cope with the loss in his own way. I am a big believer in the saying, "If it ain't broke, don't fix it". However, I would add in my conversation with the parent that sometimes teenagers have a delayed grief reaction and may experience a grief reaction at a later time. This is common among teenagers and does not mean that there is anything wrong with the youngster. It may be just too difficult or painful for him to deal with this loss at the present time. If in the interview I sense that the student's grades are slipping, the student is withdrawing from friends or becoming uncommunicative, he has stopped participating in school activities and outside interests, or that there is unusual acting out behavior going on at home or in school, then I would call the parent and share my concerns. I would recommend that the student see a mental health professional who has a background in bereavement counseling.

As noted earlier, counseling should never be forced on students. Many students in support groups have reported on how parents insist that they see a therapist. The student would be forced to attend counseling sessions where they would have little to say. It became a waste of time and money. Furthermore, they often felt resentment that the parent did not trust their own judgment in such an important matter.

STARTING A SUPPORT GROUP

The previous chapter established a short term intervention for assisting the bereaved student immediately after the loss. However, as we have learned, the bereavement process for most individuals continues for months and even years. In my experience, the best strategy to help students in the long term is the support group.

Starting a support group in the school setting presents several challenges. First and foremost is identifying students who have lost a family member. This is a much more difficult challenge than one would imagine. I have found that school records are not always accurate in this regard. Widowed or remarried spouses do not always volunteer information about a deceased parent in the student's registration forms. Furthermore, clerical staff who are responsible for updating student records often do not do so. Given this, I have resorted to a multifaceted approach. I initially run a report on the school's student information system searching for students who have lost a parent. Deceased siblings usually are not tracked in the database of student information systems so this information has to come from other sources. After I have my initial list, I then begin surveying the pupil personnel team which includes the school counselors, psychologists, social workers, and the school nurse. They are usually a good source of information on students who have lost a family member. I then survey the PPS team of the previous school which in most cases is the middle school. I have also emailed teachers asking if they know of anyone who has lost a family member.

Interestingly, the students themselves are a good source of information and I will ask them when I am interviewing students for the group. Another good source of information would be elementary principals and elementary PPS staff, but since they are several years removed from the present high school students, they may not remember all such cases. Even with this extensive effort, I have missed students who have lost a family member. My most glaring example is a student who approached me about joining the support group after our second meeting. She had lost both parents and was living with her grandparents. This information was not in the school records nor was it common knowledge among PPS staff. She learned about the group from a friend who I had interviewed for the group. One thing that I would not do is make announcements on the PA or put posters up in the school about the group. I prefer a low key approach, because the group is about a personal and sensitive matter, and it is not necessary for the entire student body to know about the group. The students in my groups appreciated my attempts to keep the group as private as possible.

One question that has come up frequently is whether students who have lost a grandparent be included in the group. In most cases, I would say no. It depends upon the type of relationship that the student had with the grandparent. Some grandparents who live with the family are almost surrogate parents to the student. They may even be the primarily caregiver when the parents are working. This is especially true in single family homes where the grandparent often takes the place of the parent who has left the home. The same would be true with an uncle living with the family or with a stepparent. If the grandparent, uncle, or stepparent is a central figure in the student's life and the relationship resembles that of a parent-child relationship, then the student should be included in the group.

Another challenge in starting a support group is determining a meeting pattern. Trying to have a group before school or after school almost never works. A group that meets after school interferes with club and sports activities. Bus students may not able to attend a group before school. If the school has an activity period during the school day where no classes are held, that is an ideal time to schedule the group. However, in my experience, very few schools have a period just dedicated for clubs and extra help. Therefore, the next best scenario is to have the group meet weekly during different periods so that the first meeting meets first period, the second meeting takes place second period and, so on. Consequently, the students will not miss any class more than one period during a marking period. This obviously is not an ideal meeting arrangement because missing academic classes like math, science, foreign language, English, and social studies may affect the student's grades in these classes. Therefore, some accommodation is necessary. If the student is scheduled to take a test on the day a group is to meet, students are instructed to report to class and take the test. Furthermore, when the group meets the period that the student has lunch, the students are told to buy/bring their lunch and report to the group a few minutes late. These are compromises that the facilitator must make when negotiating within the constraints of a school day.

Gaining the support of administrators, teachers, and other school staff is critical to the success of the group. I begin by speaking to the principal and other administrators who may be in contact with the students, explaining the purpose of the group and how the meetings are scheduled. Then, I email the teachers and briefly explain the nature of the group and that students should be permitted to attend, unless they are having a test. I will also email the homeroom teachers and explain that it is critical that passes be distributed on the day that the group will meet. When students receive the pass in homeroom, they will give it to the teacher whose class they will miss that day. The pass system is unreliable in most schools. The homeroom teacher may forget to give the pass to the student, or the student may come late to school and miss getting the pass. In cases where the teacher is absent, the substitute teacher may not check the mailbox of the teacher and not pick up the passes. It is some of these small procedural details that can undermine the effectiveness of the group. Therefore, it is important to have a system in place where the facilitator can effectively communicate with the student and the teachers. I have worked at improving the shortcomings of the pass system but there may be other more effective ways of communicating with students and teachers regarding group meetings. Each school is different and the facilitator must determine the best way of communicating for it is instrumental to the success of the group.

Deciding on when to begin the group is another important consideration. When I first began adolescent support groups, I would try to start them when the students' academic demands were lightest such as the beginning of the second semester. My thinking was that there would be fewer tests and critical assignments at the beginning of a semester and students would be less anxious about missing a class. After facilitating two groups at mid-year, one student suggested that the group might be more helpful if it met during the holiday period starting with Thanksgiving and continuing into January. Other students agreed with this idea and every group thereafter I started right after Thanksgiving. I have found that the student was correct in the timing of the group. Since holiday periods are when families gather to celebrate and participate in traditions, previous losses and painful memories tend to re-surface more during these times and there is more to talk about in the group.

Equally important is choosing the day of the week to meet. I have always avoided Mondays and Fridays since school holidays often fall on these days. Also, since many teachers give tests towards the end of the week, I have always avoided Thursdays. I then look at when school assemblies and other school wide programs are scheduled. Of the remaining days, Tuesday or Wednesday, the one that presents fewer conflicts with other school programs is the day that I will choose. One mistake I made several years ago was to schedule our first meeting on a day the school was having an AIDS awareness assembly. I had to cancel our first meeting and the following week the group had to be cancelled for some other reason. When we finally did meet on the third week, I had a very poor turnout and there was much confusion among the students, some of whom thought the group itself was cancelled. The group never really recovered from this poor beginning and consisted of only a few students. It is critical that the first few meetings take place as scheduled. If a meeting has to be cancelled after several successful meetings, I have found that the group members develop a commitment to the group and it will not be adversely affected by the cancellation.

In facilitating support groups, I always like to have at least one co-facilitator and sometimes two. I usually ask counselors, social workers, psychologists, or any other mental health professionals (especially those who have lost a parent at an early age) to join me in facilitating the group. In one school, I had two teachers in the group who both lost a parent when they were in high school. The students really enjoyed having them in the group and they contributed a great deal. The advantage to having two or three facilitators is that in case there is an emergency and one of the facilitators cannot attend, the meeting does not have to be cancelled since the other facilitator(s) can lead the group. Another advantage to multiple facilitators is that both sexes can be represented. As we learned earlier, there are gender differences in the way individuals respond to grief. Therefore, a male student may identify more with the male facilitator and female students with the female facilitator.

A final challenge to starting a group is finding a suitable meeting place. I would avoid meeting in a classroom because there are too many distractions. Teachers may come into the room to retrieve materials, students may wander in looking for a friend or teacher, and the classroom phone may ring as the main office is trying to find someone. I would suggest looking for a conference room or office that is private and away from where most students congregate. If the meeting place is in a highly visible location, other students will see the teenagers in the support group and question them as to what they are doing. Furthermore, the room should have chairs that can be moved to form a circle. Leaving chairs in a classic classroom arrangement will focus attention on the leaders as "teachers" and invite classroom behavior such as students' raising hands and expecting the leaders to "teach" a lesson. Arranging the chairs in a circle with both facilitators and students sitting together establishes an environment where all the participants are on the same level and the focus is not on any one individual. This is the best sitting arrangement for good group interaction.

Once all these organizational details have been addressed, the facilitators can begin interviewing the students to see who is interested in joining the support group. The facilitators divide up the students based on familiarity; if a facilitator knows a student, it makes sense for that person to interview the student. After all the known students have been identified, the remaining students are divided randomly. The students are given a pass to see one of the facilitators. In my experience, when the student receives a pass to see someone in the office, they immediately suspect that something is wrong, so the interview begins with a brief explanation for the purpose of the meeting. The facilitator explains to the student that with the holidays approaching, the guidance office has a special program designed to assist students who have lost a family member. The facilitator then confirms with the student that she has lost a family member. He then asks the student if she has ever been in a support group. He emphasizes that the group is not therapy. It is just a group of students getting together on a weekly basis to discuss their experiences on losing a family member. The group will have two or three leaders who are not teachers but just facilitators of the discussions. After discussing the nature and logistics of a support group, the facilitator will ask the student how the person died and when. A good follow-up question would be how the student has coped with the loss. At this point, the facilitator would not ask any further questions about the loss, because it is not advisable to turn the interview into a counseling session. Instead, the facilitator would try to determine if the student is interested in the group.

Many students whose loss occurred a long time ago may respond that they have gotten over it and do not need further assistance. With these students, I ask if they would join the group to help others whose loss may be much more recent. Some students, especially boys, may be more apt to join the group if it is under the guise of trying to help others. In this way, they do not have to admit to themselves and to others that they are really joining because they are still struggling with the loss. My experience has been that those students who join to help others often are just as needy as those who are joining to get help. If the student seems undecided about joining, the facilitator can invite the student to the first meeting and then let her decide whether she wants to remain with the group. At the end of the interview, the facilitator thanks the student and tells those who are not interested they can return if they change their minds. These students will still get information on when and where the group meets, and a reminder to see the facilitator if they decide to join.

Another important issue that often arises during these interviews is with having siblings in the same group. Ideally, it is best to have siblings in different groups so they can speak more freely. However, it would be very difficult in most schools to have enough students to form two groups. Therefore, the facilitator is left with trying to make the sibling situation work with one group.

My experience is that siblings who are two or more years apart in age do not want to be in the same group. The older sibling has a different peer group and being together in the same support group with the younger sibling becomes too awkward. However, some of my best group members have been twins or siblings who are close in age. They often have the same peer group and may be in some classes together. When siblings "hang out" together by choice, they usually are very comfortable being in the same support group. In either case, it is important to let siblings know that they would be in the same group together so they can decide what to do.

Throughout the interview, it is important to be aware of body language. Students who are still struggling with their loss may become teary-eyed, or their pain may be evident in their voice or facial expression. They should be encouraged to join, but the decision is ultimately theirs; after all, the support group is completely voluntary. Furthermore, I emphasize to students that the group is not just for newly bereaved students, as adult groups usually are. Students who have lost a parent when they were very young may have different issues than the newly bereaved student, but those issues still need to be addressed. I once had a student whose father died when he was two years old. Although his mom had remarried and he had a stable family life, he had a tremendous need to know who his father was. He was one of the most active participants and contributed greatly to the group. The other students learned from him the importance of keeping the memories alive of the deceased family member. He learned from them the importance of knowing his father by speaking to those who knew him best. Having a diverse group of students with a wide array of experiences really adds to the richness of the discussions.

After interviewing the new students, the facilitators approach the students who were in the group the previous year. It is not necessary to interview them, since the students have already been in a group and know what it is all about. They are asked if they had a good experience with the group last year, and if so would they like to be a part of the new group. Having a few of these veteran students return is very important because they tend to become leaders in the new group, and serve as role models in terms of setting the right tone for the group. It is important to have only a few so that the new group will develop its own unique character instead of being a rerun of the previous group.

For all those students who are interested in the group, both new and returning members, the facilitator advises them to speak to their parents. The facilitator gives the student a letter to be presented to his parent(s) explaining the purpose of the group and the student's interest in joining (see below).

Dear Parent or Guardian:

As we approach another holiday season, our attention focuses on students for whom the holidays may have a very different meaning. Students who have lost a family member often feel the loss more acutely this time of year. In recent years, the Guidance Department has offered a support group where students can talk to peers who have had a similar loss. In this group, students can learn from the adult leaders and from one another on how to deal with the many issues that arise in losing a family member. This is a discussion group and not therapy. Previous groups have benefited many of our students by helping them understand how the loss has affected them. We have interviewed many students and your child has expressed an interest in participating.

The group will begin in December and meet weekly for one period. Our meetings will be held during different periods each week so students will not miss any class more than once during the marking period. Students will not be penalized for missing a class; teachers will be notified that they are with us. However, they will be responsible for any work that they missed. Please sign the bottom of the letter to acknowledge that you have read it and have your student return to one of us. If you have any questions, please call at_____. Thank you.

Sincerely,
(signatures)
[Director of Guidance]   [Social Worker]   [Guidance Counselor]
Name of Student _____
Signature of Parent/Guardian _____

If the student does not return the letter within a week, which is usually the case, the facilitator who interviewed the student can follow up with a phone to the parent. This is a great opportunity to explain the group to the parent and answer any questions that she may have.

In my experience, the overwhelming majority of parents are very grateful that the school is trying to help their child. However, I have encountered resistance from some parents. The concerns expressed by these parents usually have to do with the impact of discussing the loss on the adolescent. Will discussing the deceased parent have a negative reaction on the student and cause a regression? This concern is particularly prevalent among parents who have remarried and now are trying to build a new blended family. In a sense, by having the student revisit a loss from the previous family, it becomes a threat to the new family. The implicit message is, if we do not talk about it, perhaps Mary will forget about the painful experience of losing her mother.

With such parents, I emphasize that it is a discussion group and not therapy. A teenager will never forget her biological parent, especially during the holiday season. Having an outlet for these students where they can discuss how they feel and learn that others feel the same way, provides an important source of validation. Instead of feeling that something is wrong with them for feeling a certain way, these students can feel validated by hearing others who are having similar feelings. If the resistance continues, I suggest that the student be permitted to attend once. After the meeting, the student and parent can discuss the value of the group, and they can make a joint decision on whether to continue with the group.

As mentioned in the second chapter, sometimes cultural influences come into play and/or the concern for the student is too great to permit her participation. In such cases, it is best to respect the family's wishes and not include the student in the group, even if the student wants to join.

THE FIRST MEETING
OF THE SUPPORT GROUP

A few days before the first meeting, the facilitator sends out a note to all participants confirming all the important details of the group such as the meeting time, date and location. If possible, it is helpful to check with the teachers informally or with the students themselves between periods to ascertain that the note was received. The day of the first meeting, the students will also receive a pass excusing them from the class they are going to miss. The note, informal contact with the teachers or students, and pass are all attempts to make sure that the important communication is getting through to the students.

The first meeting of any support group is always the most important because if it does not go well, the members will probably not return for the next meeting. Therefore, providing a welcoming environment where students can feel comfortable and at ease is important. Facilitators usually bring in refreshments or breakfast treats. Furthermore, if it is a large school where many of the students may not know each other, having name tags may be useful in helping both leaders and students learn names faster. The facilitators in the opening statements should welcome the students to the group and review again the nature of a support group. While this was already done in the initial interview and in the parent letter, I have found that repeating this in a large group is good practice because it is important for everyone to hear the same message. The facilitators should emphasize that students were brought together because they had a common life experience, the loss of a family member. Because of this, they probably can understand each other better than students who have not had this experience. The group is an opportunity for them to discuss common experiences and learn from each other about grief and the challenges that lie ahead for them. Therefore, it is a self-help discussion group and not therapy. Unlike a classroom, they can determine the topics since it is their group. The facilitators are not teachers but are there to simply start and lead the discussions. The facilitators invite students to ask any questions they may have about the group.

The next step is to establish a safe environment so students feel comfortable participating in the group. The facilitator asks the students what guidelines or rules are needed to make the group safe for them. The most common responses are usually confidentiality, respecting the opinion of others, giving everyone a chance to speak and etc. The facilitators can also volunteer some appropriate rules such as attendance and refraining from giving advice unless asked for. After this discussion, one of the facilitators should write a list of the agreed upon rules and ask students to sign it. This becomes a written commitment that the students are making to each other to make the group a safe place for all.

The facilitators will now ask the students to introduce themselves and share why they decided to join the group. Most students will mention the person who died in their family and when and how it occurred. Some students will volunteer that they joined the group to help others or that they joined because their parent thought it was a good idea. Regardless of the reason, all are equally welcomed to be part of the group. It is very important that all students have the opportunity to speak and introduce themselves at the first meeting so the facilitators need to be mindful of that. Some students may have a difficult time speaking and it is important that the student not feel on the spotlight when it is her turn to speak. Facilitators should monitor this carefully and say to the student, "if this is hard for you to do, we will go to the next student and return to you later". The facilitators should also participate in the introductions and share any losses that they have experienced in their lives. Even though their losses may have occurred as an adult, it helps to establish a connection with the students and puts them at the same level as the students. One of the facilitators can also take notes of this meeting which would help with the debriefing session the following day.

An alternate opening activity that works well and promotes bonding among younger adolescents (middle school age) is the broken heart. In this, the facilitator cuts out the shape of a heart from poster paper. The heart is cut up into several pieces with each student in the group receiving a piece. The students are asked to write their name on the piece of the heart they received and the person who they lost. The facilitator then collects all the pieces, tapes them together, and tells the students that they are all in the group because they have had their heart broken. They all share a common goal, that is, to mend their broken hearts. The pieced together heart becomes a metaphor for their shared grief and their journey to healing. Each student can then talk about the person that they lost. In the meetings that follow, the broken heart can be hung in a place in the room where it is visible to all as a reminder of their commonality.

Furthermore, the facilitator can suggest that the members bring in a picture of the deceased so that the group can get to know the person. Each subsequent meeting will begin with students bringing in a picture and while it is being passed around, the student can speak about the deceased family member. My experience is that some students will forget so it may take several weeks before most will bring in their pictures, and some will not bring in any pictures. Again, I do not want any student to become uncomfortable because he did not bring in a picture so it becomes a strongly encouraged but voluntary activity. Furthermore, the facilitators should also participate and bring in a picture as well. When I brought in a picture, the students seemed to appreciate that I was willing to share my loss with them.

Usually the final interaction of the first meeting deals with a discussion of the upcoming holiday season. The facilitator explains that the group was purposely scheduled to meet this time of year because the holidays often cause many old feelings to resurface. Since the first meeting is held soon after Thanksgiving, the facilitator can ask what Thanksgiving was like for them. Did the holiday bring back memories of the deceased? Were they good memories or painful memories? Another question can center on the theme of Thanksgiving which is to be grateful for all that we have. The facilitator can ask if the students felt thankful on Thanksgiving. These questions usually generate many different kinds of responses and it becomes a teachable moment. The facilitator can point out that grief is a very individual experience which accounts for the diversity of responses. We all grieve in our own very unique way and there is no right or wrong response to these questions. For those students whose Thanksgiving was a sad and painful day, the facilitator should validate their feelings by stating that it is okay to feel that way. Feelings are neither right nor wrong, but just a part of us. They often change with time.

The meeting ends with the facilitators asking the students for feedback on the first meeting. Did the students feel comfortable in the group? Is there anything that needs to be changed for the next meeting? If any students seem upset, the facilitator should see them after the group ends and before they go back to class. The facilitators should also compliment the students for the courage they have shown in joining the group. It takes a special person to come to a group and talk about a very personal experience with strangers.

The facilitators should meet after each meeting to assess what transpired in the group and plan for the next meeting. The note taker can begin by summarizing the meeting. What were the most salient issues discussed? Aside from content, observant facilitators will also discuss body language. Were there any students who seemed disinterested or uncomfortable? Were there any students who did not participate? Did any students monopolize the discussion or behave in an inappropriate manner? What adjustments need to be made to address any of these concerns? This discussion will be the basis for the planning of the next meeting. Furthermore, there should be some follow up with students who did not attend the first meeting. I have found that sometimes students could not attend for legitimate reasons such as the teacher would not let them out of class, they had a substitute teacher who forgot to give the passes out, or they could not afford to miss a core academic class. For these students, the facilitator can just give a brief summary of the first meeting and welcome them to join the next meeting. For those who missed the meeting because they have reservations about the group, the facilitator should try to discuss their concerns. If the student still has reservations, he should be dropped from the group with the understanding that the door is open to him if he changes his mind.

THE SECOND MEETING AND BEYOND

The second meeting begins with an introduction of any new members who missed the first meeting. The new students would briefly share why they wanted to join the group and the facilitator would go over the rules decided by the group to make it safe. New members can also suggest additional rules. They would be asked to sign their names to the list of rules affirming that they will abide by them. The facilitator then asks if anyone brought pictures of the deceased. Those who remembered to bring pictures will pass them around and talk about their family member. Sometimes it is helpful for a facilitator or a student who was in the group last year to begin. In this way the new students have an idea of what kind of information to provide on the deceased. Students are encouraged to ask questions as pictures are passed around. Students who forgot to bring pictures can do so the following week.

After the picture activity, the facilitator will try to generate a discussion with the students by doing a review of the week or by asking if they have any topics related to grief and bereavement that they wish to discuss. For a review of the week, the facilitator can just go around the circle and ask the students if anything of significance has occurred at school or home since the first meeting. Another variation of this activity, which may be more successful with quiet groups, is to ask each student to rate their week on a 1 to 10 and explain the reason for their rating. Since it is their group, they should determine the topics. In my experience with support groups, adolescents tend to be more guarded than adults and generally asking them to offer topics or doing a review of the week at the beginning of the group usually generates limited discussion. I have found that they need some help to get them going. Therefore, if the above questions do not produce a discussion, I will use an ice breaker especially in the first few meetings. Since students may still have questions about the death or about how the loss has impacted them, the facilitator can develop a questionnaire as shown on the next page, (Activity 1).

The questionnaire is distributed to the students. Students are asked to read the questions and identify any that they can relate to. From past experience, these questions have generated discussions on issues related to unfinished business which often include circumstances of death and degree of closure. As noted earlier in the book, many parents try to protect their children by not providing detailed information about the severity of an illness or accurate information in cases of a sudden or violent death. Consequently, these children who have incomplete or inaccurate information about the death may have made false assumptions that are not true. This can create roadblocks to the healing process. Other questions focus on the vulnerability we feel after a loss; i.e., how can we love or trust again when we know we could lose someone else we love?

The question about God often brings up religious beliefs. While religion is not a topic I would introduce, it may come up. If it does we discuss it. Most teenagers are tougher on God than their parents. They are less apt to accept an explanation such as the death was God's will. They are more likely to see contradiction in the notion of a benevolent God who allows terrible things to happen to those who they love. If this is a major issue in the group, I sometimes recommend to students Rabbi Kushner's book, <u>Why Bad Things Happen to Good People</u>. He takes a different look at the role of God in our universe and offers explanations that may be more helpful to the newly bereaved.

Questions about Loss

1. Why did this have to happen to me?
2. I still have questions about what happened. Who should I go to for answers?
3. Was it my fault?
4. Could I have stopped it?
5. What do you say to someone who is dying?
6. Who else will I lose?
7. Will I ever feel normal again?
8. Will I laugh again?
9. How could God let this happen?
10. What should we do with his personal belongings?
11. Will I ever love again?
12. How can I trust?
13. My question is _____

If students cannot relate to any questions on the list, they are asked to write their own question. Again, this sends the important message that grief is a very individual experience and that there are many other good questions that the bereaved can have that do not appear on the list. Students with their own questions can read them to the group and generate additional discussions.

Another very effective ice breaker is a survey of common feelings experienced after a loss. This can be done by simply creating a handout as shown on Activity 2. Students are asked to circle any feelings that they are experiencing. Additionally, they are asked to write in feelings that are not on the list. The facilitator then asks the students to share those feelings which are the strongest. This activity can generate a great discussion on how feelings are impacted by grief. While students will be experiencing many common feelings associated with grief most will have some very unique feelings that are not being experienced by others. This reinforces the concept that grief is very individual and unique. The discussion can also explore the triggers that cause emotions to surface such as old pictures, music, and the deceased's personal belongings, as well as how to manage feelings when they become overwhelming.

If students have lost their family member long ago, there is a variation of the activity that may be more meaningful for them. For these students, the facilitator can ask them to circle or write in how they felt after the death and then on a duplicate copy of the activity how they feel now. The students can compare to see how their feelings have changed over time.

» ACTIVITY 2

What Feelings have You Experienced since Your loss?

fear	peaceful	abandonment
shock	numb	rejection
appreciation	successful	melancholy
anger	loved	outraged
guilt	depression	confident
regret	lonely	overwhelmed
confusion	happy	inferior
relief	rejection	different
exhaustion	worried	lost
sad	hopeful	envious

Additional feelings _____

This can then become the focus of the discussion, that is, why our feelings change. It is a great way to show students how grief is a dynamic process and that as we heal our feelings, thoughts, and perspective evolve and change.

As the second meeting comes to a close, the facilitator should do a quick debriefing to make sure that the students are in a good state of mind and are ready for their next class. If a student is upset, she may need some private debriefing with a facilitator before going back to class, even if it means being late. This should become a standard practice. Part of feeling safe in a group is knowing that people will be there to assist you if the discussion triggers an emotional reaction.

The third and succeeding meetings begin the same way. Students who have pictures will share them and there will be a review of the week followed by suggested topics offered by students. Again, if these do not generate a discussion, the facilitator should introduce an activity to help students get started. Aside from ice breakers, another effective tool is the use of poems or letters written either by published authors or by other students. One poem that is particularly relevant to the holiday season is "The Elephant in the Room" which appears on Activity 3.

The facilitator distributes a copy of the poem to the students and asks for a volunteer to read it aloud. After the reading, the facilitator begins a discussion on the meaning of the poem and if the students were ever in a situation where they felt like the writer. Most students that I have worked with can relate to the poem, and they share instances of when this happened to them. When students report that there is little discussion in their own family of the deceased family member, the facilitator can make this part of the discussion. In most families, there are those who cope with loss by not thinking about it, while other family members have a real need to talk about the deceased. This can create communication barriers as we saw with GL's family. What can a teenager in such a family do? One of the ideas usually discussed is having students bring the poem home and placing it where it is very visible to all. Perhaps as others read it, the poem can become part of a family discussion and thus begin to break down the communication barriers. The discussion can be extended to family gatherings that take place during the holidays.

During these festive occasions, people are often reluctant to mention the deceased, fearing that the immediate family members will become upset and a happy occasion would be spoiled. However, if a family member of the deceased breaks the ice by sharing a fond memory of the deceased, it gives others permission to talk about the deceased. It can become a warm heartfelt occasion where everyone can join in sharing of the great memories rather than spending an awkward evening with the elephant in the room.

At the end of the discussion, the facilitator can invite students to bring in poems, stories or letters that they have read or written. In the groups that I have facilitated, many students have accepted this invitation and brought in some exceptional poems or letters honoring the deceased family member. Some of the best and most moving college entrance essays that I have read came from seniors who wrote about a deceased parent. When students have brought in their own writing and read it to the group, it has usually created a tremendous bonding experience because group members can relate to the student. It reinforces the connection that they have with one another and creates additional topics for discussion.

» ACTIVITY 3

The Elephant in the Room

There is an elephant in the room
It is large and squatting, so it is hard to get
around it.
Yes we squeeze by with, "How are you" and "I'm Fine."
And a thousand other forms
of trivial chatter.
We talk about the weather.
We talk about work.
We talk about everything–
except the elephant in the room.

There is an elephant in the room.
We all know that it is there.
We are thinking about the elephant
as we talk together.
It is constantly on our minds.
For you see, it is a very big elephant.
It has hurt us all.
But we do not talk about the
elephant in the room.
Oh please, say her name
Oh please, say "Barbara" again

Oh please, let's talk about the
elephant in the room.
For if we talk about her death,
Perhaps we can talk about her life?
Can I say "Barbara" to you and not
have you look away
For if I cannot, then you are leaving me
Alone...
In a room...
With an elephant...

Terry Kettering

If no one in the group brings in writing pieces, the facilitator can use poems, letters, and essays written by students from previous groups. Of course, this should be done with the permission of the student who wrote the piece and that person should remain anonymous to the members of the current group. If this is not an option (there are no written pieces from a previous group or the author would prefer that his writing not be shared with the group), GL's poem in Activity 4 can be used. It can be a very effective springboard for discussion, because her poem reveals so many themes related to loss. The facilitator can begin by distributing a copy of the poem to the students and asking for a volunteer to read it. After the reading, the facilitator asks if the students can identify with any of the feelings that GL expressed in her poem. Which of these feelings had the greatest impact on them? Are they still struggling with these feelings now? In what ways are their experiences with loss different from hers? Some key talking points would be GL's struggle to accept the reality of her father's death; the changes that have taken place in her life and family; her sense of protest and unfairness in losing a loved one; the special relationship and love she had for her father; and the great memories she has of him. Furthermore, the issue she brings up about the family no longer eating together is a great point for discussion. I have found that the majority of students who lose a parent do not eat dinner together. Many students eat in front of their television, computer, or just eat alone in their room. As we discussed earlier, death can pull a family together or apart, and certainly it will facilitate the latter if everyone is eating alone. Therefore, it is a good to have a discussion on the importance of spending time together.

Finally, GL speaks in the 10th line about her great need to let her feelings out in the poem. The facilitator can ask the students if they feel that writing about the deceased and their grief would be helpful to them. Writing can be a great outlet for stress and sorrow, and helps students sort out their feelings to gain a better understanding of their own grief experience. Students who wish can also bring their writing to the group. Of course, this is all voluntary and should not be presented as an assignment.

» ACTIVITY 4

GL's Poem

As I sit in my room thinking, I wonder how could this be?
Why does it have to be this way?

Why are we here and he's not?
Why is he there and we're not?
I ask this question a thousand times a day.
I still can't figure it out.
Why is life this way?
Why are the ones we love not always with us?
How could things like this happen?
I've been keeping all these feelings in but it's time to let them out.
I never knew you could miss someone so much.
It does not feel or seem real.
It seems like a dream.
A dream that keeps going.
I play the same game over and over again with myself.
When I'm home and he is not, I say he's at work.
When I'm at work and he is not, I say he is home.
At dinner I do not know what to think.
We used to eat dinner as a family
But, now everyone eats dinner when they feel.
I can't believe that something like this can happen.
How could something so good go away?
One day he just disappeared.
Sort of like a magic show but this is different.
The thing that is different is that they come back in magic shows and
He's never coming back
It is so hard to face.
He was there when we needed him.
He was never unfair.
He cared.
Even though he was not home during the day,
He made up for it when he got home.
He used to walk in and say, "I'm home did anybody miss me?"
Some days I still feel like I hear these words.
But, I know that it is my imagination.

I remember all the games we all used to play when I was younger.
He was always there for us and never let us down.
It's weird how someone so special is never going to come back.
It's weird how so many things are never gonna be the same.
I remember in the summer how we used to play volleyball for hours.
We used to play tag and have water fights.
Whenever I fell or got hurt, he used to sing this certain song to me.
Or he'd just say I hope you did not crack my patio.
So I'd laugh.
I can go on forever about this very special man.
This man is my father.
I just can't explain how much I love him and I'll never forget
all the good times
I just hope he knows how much I love him and how much I miss him.
He's the greatest dad and will always be in my heart.
I hope he feels no pain and knows that me and the rest of his
family and friends love him.

For students who do not respond well to writing or reading poems, letters or stories, there are other media that can be used to generate discussion. I once participated in an art therapy exercise on grief where the participants were asked to assemble a collage of pictures telling about some loss in their life. The pictures, which were distributed throughout the room in piles, were random cutouts from magazines. Some pictures were nature scenes, others were about people, and still others were advertisements. Some cutouts had no pictures at all but were just words or sayings. In a quiet environment with soothing music, the students in the class arranged the pictures and glued them on poster paper. After about 30 minutes of doing this art project, students displayed their poster and told their story through the pictures. It was incredible to see how some quiet students became very verbal and told very intricate stories about a pet, friend, or family member who had died.

In my next meeting, I asked the students if they would be interested in doing such a project. The students were very interested in doing it. I had the facilitator with whom I had done the exercise come to the group. She did the activity with some modification; I did not want the art project to become a therapy session. The students assembled and glued the pictures on a poster. As they finished, the facilitator would hang up the postures on the wall. Each student then explained his picture and told a wonderful story about the deceased family member. Some of the more quiet students who never brought in a picture of their loved one had some of the most elaborate posters. For these students, art was a better medium to express their loss than using ice breakers or written pieces. Therefore, I would recommend this as an activity but it is best done with a trained practitioner who would avoid interpreting or analyzing the posters since that would transcend the boundaries of a discussion group.

The last meeting before the holiday recess in an important one and has a structured agenda. The facilitator begins with a discussion of the students' plans for the holidays, including their holiday traditions. I have found that teenagers want to still celebrate traditions such as gift giving, decorating the home, and writing and collecting holiday cards. I have learned from adult support groups that parents would prefer to skip the holidays or at least have them pass as quickly as possible. Students are encouraged to think about finding a middle ground with their parents. How can family traditions be modified to make them a bit easier for parents, but still enjoyable for the children? This is where students who were in the group the previous year can be of great help. Since they have experienced the holidays at least once since the death, they may be able to share what they did the previous year to help the entire family have a more enjoyable holiday season. Another important issue is how the deceased is memorialized in these family traditions. As the research points out, continuing bonds with the deceased is very important for teenagers. Many have very creative ways of remembering the deceased, such as wearing something with special meaning or by doing some special act. One set of twins I had in a group would write a note each Christmas to their dad. They would put the note in a balloon, fill it up with helium, and let it rise into the sky. It was their way of staying connected with their dad. The facilitator can also share a prayer or poem that can be read by the student at the family dinner or at the beginning of a holiday tradition. Below is a prayer that I received from a man who was in one of my support groups. It has proven to be very popular with both adults and students with whom I have worked.

I Am Still Near

Death has taken me from this world,
and though we are apart, I am still near,
All that we meant to each other remains true,
in trust and faith, have no fear.

Keep me always close to your heart!
For I leave with you what no one can steal,
a treasure chest of precious, happy memories:
the tender, loved filled moments we shared,
as well as the challenging times
that brought us together

When you are in need,
speak to me, call my name.
I will come to you with wisdom and light,
To fill your soul with peace,
and guide you in the pathways that
lead to life forever with our Loving God.

I also offer you this sacred promise:
when I am home in God's embrace,
whenever you call on me,
I will still be present to you,
for neither death nor grave can break the
bonds of love that we on earth once knew.

The poem is written from the perspective of the deceased speaking to the living. A good point of discussion would be how the members would reply to the deceased. They could even write their own poem in response.

A great way to close the meeting is for the facilitator to give the students in the group a small gift. Students will appreciate the thought and gesture. One year I gave them a copy of Earl Grollman's book, <u>Straight Talk About Death for Teenagers</u>. It is an excellent book that is short, concise, informative, and written on a level that teenagers can easily understand. He begins with an explanation of what grief is, how it makes us feel, and gives practical suggestions on managing grief. Other topics he covers include different relationship losses (parent, grandparent, sibling, and friend), circumstances of death, coping with loss, and rebuilding a new life without the deceased. The book does a great job of demystifying grief and clarifying much of what they may not understand. It can serve as a nice bridge for them during the holidays, when the group is not meeting, and it can become a topic for discussion for when the group resumes.

AFTER THE HOLIDAYS

The first meeting after the holidays is a great opportunity for the students to examine their reactions during the holiday season. The facilitator can begin by asking students for feedback on their holiday events and activities. What were their best moments? What were their most difficult moments? Are they happy or sad that the holidays are over? Most important, what did they learn that could help them with future holidays? This last question is indicative of an important shift in the focus of the group. In the beginning and middle meetings, the focus was on learning about grief and dealing with the holidays. Now the focus will be on the future and applying what they have learned to make their lives better. Most teenagers and adults feel powerless when they lose a loved one. They could not stop the events or illness that led to the death of the loved one and they experience a loss of control. Consequently, the facilitator can use empowerment strategies to restore a sense of control over their own lives. Many of the newly bereaved develop important personal qualities and strengths in coping with their loss. Here are some good questions to address: Is there any good that can come from losing someone you really love? How can this unfortunate experience somehow help you later in life? Many students reply that the loss has made them become more responsible and mature. For those who have lost a parent, they have had to become more self-sufficient because the surviving parent cannot do it all. Many have had to assume more house chores and help out with younger siblings. They are also more appreciative of the important people in their lives and resent peers who complain or say that they hate their parents. For those who have lost a sibling, many have been able to assist the parents by doing more around the house, or by being more open to compromise when there is a conflict in the family. By acknowledging their growth and resilience, the facilitator can empower students and restore a sense of control over their lives.

At this stage of the group, students are usually more comfortable and will bring up topics for discussion. There is less need for ice-breakers and structured activities, but it is always good to have something in case the discussion breaks down. Sometimes, other topics emerge unrelated to grief such as mid-term exams, scheduling and college planning. It is appropriate to discuss topics not related to grief, because sometimes students need a break from the intensity of grief. Also, it is a sign that they are feeling more upbeat. With the wisdom that they have gained in the group, students are encouraged to reach out and help others. For instance, occasionally during the course of the group, a student suffers the loss of a family member. The facilitator can discuss this with the group to see if anyone would like to reach out to the student. As noted earlier, the counselor or social worker usually interviews the student upon return to school. For most students, it is much too soon to join a group. However, some students with a very recent loss are looking for the support that a group can provide. In such cases, students are allowed to come to a meeting to judge for themselves if the group is right for them. In my most recent group, one of the members knew a student who had just lost her father. She approached her about the group and volunteered to accompany her to the next meeting. The student was very appreciative to have a "buddy" at her first meeting, and everyone in the group made her feel welcome. During the meeting, it was great to see how the other group members reached out to the student and offered her encouragement and hope. If the student is not ready, she will be invited by the facilitator to join the group the following year.

Another way that the group can reach out to other needy youngsters is through the school newspaper. In my last group, one of the students was a writer for the school newspaper and I encouraged her to write an article on the group. After getting input from the group and interviewing me, she wrote a great article about the value of the group and the importance of not being afraid to reach out for help. It was very beneficial to this student who was generally quiet and shy in the group. She also read the article to the group so it could be beneficial to all and it became part of the discussion for that meeting. The article is below.

MHS Support Group
By Tara Gruber

Most people think of the holidays as happy and memorable times, spent with mom, dad, brothers, sisters and other loved ones. Others who have lost a parent or sibling do not think of holidays this way. Those selected few feel alone, secluded, and surrounded with unhappiness. There is now an empty spot at the dinner table, a piece of their heart has gone missing. After losing a loved one, many changes, problems, and emotions that have never been felt before have now emerged and dealing with them can be difficult.

Having lost a parent or sibling is possibly the most painful experience one can endure. Living everyday feeling like something is missing, something isn't right. Many people feel uncomfortable discussing their thoughts and feelings with anyone at all. You are not alone; there are quite a few students who have lost a parent or sibling who are feeling just as you are.

There is a solution to lessen the pain you are feeling, and help you to grieve in a healthier way. Some of the students here at MHS take part in the school's support group. Although many students may not be aware of this, MHS offers a special group for students who have lost a parent or sibling. Mr. Sabatini, the Director of Guidance, is the head of the group who is present every meeting as well as social worker, Mrs. Waters and guidance counselor, Mrs. Parkes.

The support group is not great in size, but this year's group is fairly large, consisting of twelve students in comparison to last year's group, which only consisted of seven.

The group usually begins after Thanksgiving when the holidays start approaching. "Around the holidays kids tend to get upset and sad when they think about the person", Mr. Sabatini said. This is absolutely true, for after losing a loved one, holidays are never the same. It usually does get very hard to remain emotionally stable during these times when all you think about is your mother, father, brother or sister who isn't with you any longer but should be spending holidays with you. During these meetings, students talk about how to handle these tough times during the year and compare often mutual thoughts relating to their lost loved ones.

I took part in this group last year and it helped me talk about subjects that I would feel uncomfortable talking about with my friends and even family. The support group helps you to open up to what you have been holding in and to talk about anything at all.

"Sometimes kids feel isolated; they feel like they are the only ones who have lost loved ones", Mr. Sabatini said. Knowing that you are not the only one makes you feel less lonely and lets you know that this did not happen to only you, but has happened to several of your peers as well. For me, it is a bit different because I have lost a brother, but most of the students in the group have lost a parent and they can relate to each other very well. We compare how our holidays are, how we feel, and what has changed at home since the loss of our loved one.

Sometimes tears are shed during these meetings, and it becomes hard to talk about certain subjects, but everyone knows that everything said is strictly confidential. Nothing leaves the room. In order to have this group exist, there needs to be trust among the students, and in this group there certainly is a massive amount of trust. No one is judged and everyone is there to listen and talk about what is going on at home or school and how to cope with his or her loss.

"Being in the group doesn't mean anything is wrong with you. It's a way of reaching out for help," Mr. Sabatini said. You aren't weird or different; it's just a way of helping yourself to be a happier person. If you are interested in joining or have any questions about the group at all, just stop by the guidance office and ask Mr. Sabatini, Mrs. Waters, Mrs. Parkes, or even me about it. New members are always welcome. Honestly, it is really a great way to discuss with your own peers how it feels to have lost one of the closest people to you, and I very much recommend this group to the students here who have lost a parent or sibling.

* * *

Usually by this stage of the group, the students have been questioned by curious parents or siblings on what is being discussed in the group. The facilitator may have also received some phone calls from parents wanting to know how their child is doing in the group. If this is a cohesive group where the members have developed trust in each other, one meeting can be set aside where each student can bring a family member. This obviously presents several challenges. Many teenagers are afraid that their parents are going to say something that will embarrass them, so there is initially resistance to this idea. Also, since so many parents work, it needs to be done in the late afternoon or early evening which presents scheduling problems. If the facilitator can work out the logistics and if students are open to trying, it can be a very beneficial experience for both the student and family member. I have been able to accomplish this only twice but both times were among the best meetings that I have ever facilitated.

The facilitator should instruct the students to bring a family member who they are concerned about or who has expressed an interest in the group. The meeting begins with a quick introduction and welcome by the facilitator as well as a review for the guests of the rules of the group. The facilitator can begin the discussion with one question that serves as an ice breaker. It can even be a sentence completion exercise such as, "I become concerned when you_____." Both student and family member will complete the statement. After everyone responds, it becomes an open dialogue where family members can ask students questions and vice versa. If there is some resistance or awkwardness in asking questions, the facilitator can have both students and family members write the questions anonymously on an index card. The facilitator then collects the cards and reads them aloud. In both instances that I have facilitated this activity, it really opened communications between students and family members. Participants from both sides gain a better understanding of how the other side experiences grief and how they deal with it. The facilitator can then end the meeting by summarizing the key points that surfaced during the interaction.

THE FINAL MEETINGS
OF THE SUPPORT GROUP

With adolescent support groups, I do not begin the group by announcing a predetermined number of meetings. I find that some groups take much longer to build a sense of trust and bonding than others. Remember that these students are all part of the same school community, and some know each other which could be a positive or negative depending upon their prior relationship. Therefore, I prefer to ask them at different points of the group if they would like to continue. The first such occasion would be right after the holidays and before midterm exams. There is usually a break in the group because of exams, so it is a good time to do an assessment. I will ask the students if they have found the group to be valuable and if they would like to continue. If the group would like to end, we agree upon a final meeting. The vast majority of groups that I have facilitated want to continue. Another assessment would be done right before a vacation break such as winter recess or spring recess. Another point to consider ending the group would be if the group is getting smaller because students have stopped attending. Regardless of when the group ends, it is always with feedback from the students. If some students would like further help after the group ends, the facilitator should make them aware that individual help is still available to them.

One of the most effective closing activities that I have developed is a student survey on how grieving students should be treated by school staff. Teachers have often approached me for advice on what to say to a recently bereaved student, or what adjustments to make to his school work. As was discussed earlier in this book, we are a death phobic society and learn little about grief in our formal education. Thus, we grow up as poorly informed adults. I begin the activity by saying to students that they have taught us, the facilitators, a great deal about what is like to lose a family member at such a young age. Perhaps they can share their wisdom to help teachers better understand grieving students. Students are always eager to participate. It is another great opportunity to make them feel empowered as they will be teaching their teachers about adolescent grief. The survey is listed below.

Advice for Teachers and Other School Staff

- Who in the school should know that the student has lost a family member?
- Should teachers come to the wake or visit the student and family?
- What should teachers say the first time they see the student?
- When the student first returns to school, what could the school do to help?
- What adjustments, in any, should teachers make to the student's school work?
- What do you think about everyone offering condolences on the student's first day back in school?
- What, if anything, should the school do to prepare the student's classmates?
- What other suggestions do you have for teachers?

Before students begin writing their responses, I encourage them to discuss each question so they can reflect on their experiences and write thoughtful answers. Furthermore, the discussion serves as a nice summary activity for the group as many of our previous discussions are revisited, and their personal growth since the beginning of the group becomes very evident. At the end of the meeting, the questionnaires are collected and reviewed. One facilitator writes a draft memo to the faculty summarizing the student's feedback and shares it with the other facilitators who can also add to it. The draft is then shown to the students at the final meeting regular meeting of the group. Students can read it, revise, and clarify if needed. When everyone feels satisfied with the memo, it is copied and distributed to the entire school staff including teachers, support personnel, and administrators. In every school that I have done this, staff members were appreciative and some thanked the facilitators for providing them with such useful information. Below is the most recent memo given to staff.

What We Learned from the Support Group

We started a support group in early December for students who have lost a family member, for most it was the loss of a parent. We met for a total of five months. The students taught us so much about life, adversity, and coping with the death of a loved one. We wanted to share with you what we learned so that you would benefit as well.

One of the things that we learned is that students regard the death of a family member as a personal and private matter. Most participants felt that those closest to the student like his teachers, counselor, coach, and close friends should be informed, but the entire school does not need to know. The students taught us that the first day back to school after the loss of a loved one is overwhelming. Well-meaning teachers, counselors, and other staff all want to offer condolences. Students are very uncomfortable with all the attention and would prefer that the first day back be as normal as possible. Perhaps a "welcome back" and "we missed you" would suffice on the first day, followed by a more formal expression of sympathy a few days or even a few weeks later. Most of the students advised to keep it simple; "I am sorry to hear about your loss" and "if you need anything, I am here for you" were two responses that they found comforting. Most of the students did not feel it was necessary for the teacher to prepare the classmates for his return to school.

Interestingly, when asked if students should be excused from school work for a period of time after the loss, most students felt that they should be expected to still do school work but be given additional time. One group member noted that it is very important for the student to have structure and a routine during this very difficult time.

Teachers and other staff are often conflicted as to whether or not they should attend the wake of the family member. The students gave different opinions on this, but most felt it depended on the relationship that the teacher has with the student. Students appreciated seeing teachers and other staff who they knew well at the wake, but they felt awkward if they really did not know the person.

One of the reoccurring themes in our discussions was that since grief is a very individual experience, avoid making assumptions. What may be helpful to one grieving student may not be helpful to all grieving students. It is best to ask the student directly what school actions are truly beneficial and which are not. This normally comes from Guidance or Pupil Personnel.

Just as a footnote; a few of our group members spoke during Awareness Week. They shared their stories of grief and how they continue to cope. The students who attended this workshop seemed to have benefited from this discussion. It even encouraged other students in the building to seek help from our staff who are dealing with loss.

If you have any questions, feel free to speak to any of us.

***

It is always important to end the group on a happy note. Therefore, the facilitators should arrange for the last meeting to be a special treat. For instance, they could take the group out for lunch at a local eatery. At this last gathering, the discussion is more informal and social than previous meetings. The facilitators try to get some feedback on the group, including if any changes need to be made for the next group. Many of the underclassmen indicate an interest in returning next year to help others. Sometimes I have used this last meeting as an opportunity to see if any students would be interested in speaking at a graduate course, Counseling for Death, Dying and Bereavement, that I teach at Hofstra University.

I have taught this course several times and have always had students willing to speak on the topic of helping children/adolescents cope with grief. The students are given a specific role, which becomes the focus of the discussion. Before their presentation, the high school and graduate students view an excellent video produced by Alan Wolfelt, "A Child's View of Grief ". The video serves as a springboard for the students who were in the support group to speak about their own loss and grief process, as well as their adjustment to living in a world without the deceased. The graduate students then ask them questions about their grief experience. The class is always a highlight of the course. The graduate students are always amazed by the courage, poise, and wisdom of these young high school students. These youngsters from the group now have become teachers of graduate students in a school counseling program. Victor Frankl, a concentration camp survivor during World War II, wrote a very powerful book on his life in concentration camps, Man's Search for Meaning. He observed that many people died when they gave up hope, while others persevered under the most extreme adversity. Frankl discovered that the ultimate goal of the survivor should be to find meaning in one's suffering. These students have found meaning in their loss by helping their support group facilitators, teachers, peers, and graduate students better understand how to help youngsters like themselves.

At the last school where I worked, there was a special program for students called Awareness Week. In March of each year, the social worker and guidance counselor who co-facilitated the group with me organized this program. It consisted of a series of workshops for students over the course of a few days on topics such as drinking and driving, substance abuse, recognizing depression, and other related adolescent issues. One year, they surveyed the students in the group to see if any might be interested in doing a workshop on loss. Several students were genuinely interested and four students volunteered to be presenters. After being prepped by the facilitators, the students gave three workshops on the same day. In a large classroom full of their peers and teachers, they each told their personal stories; discussed the level of support that they received from family and peers; spoke about their involvement in the support group; and gave the audience some great suggestions on how to be helpful to students who lost a loved one. It was an extremely genuine and courageous presentation by the students and many in the audience were moved by it. The students reported to us afterwards that many peers and teachers who attended the workshop complimented them on their courage and willingness to share their personal story to help others gain a better understanding of loss. The written evaluations at the end of the program indicated that the audiences really loved their presentation and really gained much respect for these students. This feedback was shared with the students at our meetings. These students were not only empowered by the activity but in a sense became role models for others to emulate.

THE DEATH OF A STUDENT

Few events in the life of a high school create as much distress, disruption, and pain as the death of a student. Sudden, traumatic, and violent deaths (car accidents, suicide, homicide, gang violence) are particularly intense and disruptive. News of the event usually creates a crisis atmosphere which pervades the school for several days. The school becomes paralyzed as teaching, learning and other activities come to a halt. Teachers, counselors, and administrators struggle with their own feelings of grief, while trying to help students with their own shock and pain. In recent years, schools have done a much better job of developing procedures to manage the crisis and to more quickly restore a sense of normalcy. I would like to summarize the best practices of schools that I have observed in dealing with the death of a student.

Assembling a crisis team of key staff members is the first and most important step in crisis management. The team usually consists of the principal, one assistant principal, the pupil personal services director, counselors, psychologists, social workers, nurse, dean, and a teacher in a leadership position. Smaller schools that may not employ such an extensive staff will have a smaller team. The information regarding the death of a student is usually first received from the family or police. The family should be kept apprized of all steps being taken by the school in dealing with the crisis. The principal begins by calling for a meeting of the crisis team. If the event occurs during a weekend or after school hours, the principal will call each member at home and convene an early morning meeting for the next school day. At the meeting, only factual information is shared about the student's death. Team members should refrain from speculating or theorizing about the circumstances surrounding the death for it may lead to false rumors. The team then develops a plan for the day which includes how teachers and students are notified; what support services that are needed for students and staff; a referral system for following up with students who are most impacted by the loss; and a system for communicating with parents and community/religious groups who work with students.

The principal then convenes a faculty meeting before the school day begins where members of the team share the facts regarding the student's death. The staff will have many questions but only what is factual should be shared. Then, the plan for notifying the students should be discussed with the teachers. Before the student notification process begins, relatives and close friends of the student should be removed from class and informed in a more private setting. In large schools with thousands of students, it may be best if the principal reads a statement on the school's public address system. In smaller schools, a more personal approach may be possible where a member of the team visits each class the first period and reads the statement. In either case, a member of the pupil personnel team should review with the faculty the wide range of reactions they are likely to see from students. It should be emphasized that grief is a very individual experience and that there is no correct way to grieve. Therefore, the faculty needs to respect students' reactions. Furthermore, teachers should be given guidelines on what to do with students who are too upset to remain in class and on what their role should be in class that day, i.e. should they attempt to teach their lesson? Equally important, teachers should note students who are extremely upset and notify the team so that there can be appropriate follow-up. Teachers who had the student in one of their classes may need more support from the team because these students are likely to be the ones most impacted by the death. The student's empty desk will be very upsetting to many in the class. The team should offer to have a counselor, social worker, or psychologist join the teacher in each of the deceased's classes to serve as a resource and for support.

After faculty and students are notified, parents and community/religious members should receive a mass communication, perhaps via email, of the facts regarding the student's death. This communication should also include the actions taken by the school to assist the students. Furthermore, it is best to invite parents and community members to an evening meeting where they can be advised on how to deal with their children. This is particularly important in cases of sudden and/or violent death where the shock is greatest and where there is likely to be media coverage. My experience with the media is that if you have several staff members answering questions about the death or the school's efforts to help the students, there are going to be different explanations and inconsistencies will emerge. Therefore, it is best that one member of the school administration be designated to answer all questions from reporters.

At the end of the first day, the team should meet again to assess the crisis plan. How did the students respond to the terrible news and were the school's procedures effective in managing the crisis? Typically, students will congregate in small groups throughout the day and often want to be by themselves rather than with adults. This is acceptable behavior, but the team should review the designated places where students are congregating to assure that there is sufficient supervision. In one school where I worked, students left the school building without being signed out by a parent, which made the day even more stressful and chaotic. Another important item of this meeting would be an update on information regarding the death and, if available, the viewing hours and funeral arrangements. Furthermore, students who were referred for follow-up should be discussed and appropriate interventions should be determined. Students who have faced serious personal challenges such as depression, substance abuse, and those who have suffered prior losses, should be monitored. This would also be a good time to plan an evening meeting, if needed, for parents. Finally, teachers should be apprised of any important decisions or modifications in the game plan for the next day.

The team should meet again the second day to discuss any new issues or events that may have surfaced. Any new information should be shared with the team and faculty. Another important item to address is how to support the students who plan on attending the wake, funeral, or memorial services. It is wise to have a member of the crisis team at the funeral home during viewing hours to assist any students who are extremely anxious or upset. While their presence is important, team members should respect the privacy of students and intervene only when needed. Follow-ups with students and staff who have been greatly impacted by the death should continue.

Usually, a return to normalcy will not take place until after the funeral. The day of the funeral is usually a very emotional day with many students, teachers, and other staff missing part of the school day to attend the ceremony. Students and staff who return to school are usually emotionally drained, and the entire school is impacted by this very sad day. The funeral marks the emotional climax of the crisis and usually the next school day there is a palpable lessening of emotions as the school climate begins to return to normal.

As normalcy begins to return, many students will channel their energies to memorialize their friend so that he will not be forgotten. The school newspaper and yearbook may carry pictures and articles. Bulletin boards in the halls may be turned to collages telling his life story. There may be a place designated in the school or outside where students may leave flowers, letters, and personal paraphernalia with special meaning. School sponsored functions may include a tribute to the student. Students, along with the deceased's family, may get involved in fundraising events to start a scholarship in the student's name or to purchase something for the school in memory of the student. These are all very healthy expressions of grief which should be supported by the school and the student's family.

Memorializing a student becomes more complicated for the school when the student's death involves suicide or an illegal activity such as drunk driving. Suicide does have a contagion effect where very fragile students are prone to "copycat" the act if they perceive that it was glorified. This has led to some very significant changes by the media on how suicides are reported. Similarly, if a student has been killed in a car accident because he was drunk, and injured or killed others as well, how does the school honor the student? These are philosophical questions that have no absolute answers. Some mental health professionals feel that all students should be treated the same regardless of the cause of death. In their view, not having the same memorial activities gives the message that the student's life was not valued or that we should sweep suicidal deaths under the rug. School administrators, however, are usually very concerned with the message this approach gives other students. They do not want to appear to be condoning or ignoring an act that was so wrong. One school that I worked for found a middle ground by letting the students honor the deceased in student publications or student initiated activities. However, the school would not pay tribute to the student in school sponsored functions (such as awards ceremonies), but preferred to have just a respectful moment of silence.

One final note, many schools have opted to have outside mental health agencies come into the school immediately after the death of a student to manage the crisis. Grief counselors from various agencies will often establish stations throughout the school, and reach out to students and staff who are upset or referred to them by school personnel. My experience with this has been that students often feel that the death of a classmate is a very personal and private matter. As noted earlier, most prefer to grieve with their peers than with adults. If these grief counselors are strangers to the students, some may feel resentful that outsiders are "invading" their school during this very sensitive and vulnerable time. The feeling of crisis is heightened in their minds at a time when they are looking for familiarity and assurance. If the students know the outside counselors, it would certainly mitigate this feeling. Nevertheless, it is best that the crisis is managed by the school's crisis team. Most schools have the resources and trained staff to develop and implement an effective crisis plan. If they do not have sufficient training, it should be provided during professional development hours. Any school crisis requires control and fast developing secondary events require quick and coordinated responses. When outside agencies are given a leading role in crises management, the school may be forfeiting important control and it may stymie the ability of the school to respond quickly to unfolding events.

Certainly, outside agencies can play an important supportive role, especially in cases where the school is lacking in resources. The agency should function as a member of the crisis team, providing important input and consultation. However, its role needs to be defined by the team, and if agency personnel are working with students, it should be in collaboration with the school's staff.

CASE STUDIES ON TEENAGE SUICIDE

Suicide is the seconding-leading cause of death among high school students. As noted in the previous chapter, suicide presents many challenges for schools struggling to deal with the aftermath of a student's death. In my 37 years as an educator, I experienced the death of a student by suicide on three occasions. In all three cases, I witnessed first-hand how the school tried different strategies to manage the crisis by balancing the needs of grieving students with the needs of the larger school community. This chapter is about the lessons I learned.

The first case study involved a middle school student. Kevin began his middle school career as a 7th grader in a special education self-contained class. He spent his four academic classes with the same ten students and was mainstreamed in the non-academic areas such as physical education, home economics, and art. Kevin came to the school with a long history of academic, social, and psychological problems, which seemed to be managed in his elementary school setting. In a middle school, however, where he switched classes and was exposed to many more students and teachers than he was accustomed to, he quickly began to unravel. He became disruptive in his mainstream classes and was often sent to the office by teachers who could not deal with him. Even in his special education class, he fought frequently with his peers and the teacher had to try many different strategies just to keep him in class. As the school year progressed, his behavior worsened. Sometimes, when he was removed from class, he would sit on the floor outside the classroom and sway back and forth hitting his head on the wall behind him. Kevin was very verbal about his unhappiness with the school. He would speak to me, the principal, his teachers, and basically anyone who would listen. He would verbalize his unhappiness and say that he wished that he was dead without discussing any specific plans.

Kevin lived with his father, who was at first very cooperative with the school. However, after several meetings where he had to take time off from work, he started to become resentful and began to blame the school for Kevin's problems. By mid-year, he was convinced that the school was not able to meet Kevin's needs, so he transferred him to another school district where he could have a fresh start. Sadly, there was a palpable sense of relief with Kevin's departure. His needs were too great and we did not have the programs or resources to work with him effectively.

***

A few months later, rumors began spreading around the school that Kevin had killed himself. After conferring with the principal, I called the counselor at his new school who was very shaken and confirmed that Kevin had hanged himself in his garage at the age of 12. Even with all his emotional problems, it was shocking to hear of someone so young taking his life. The school administrators conferred with central office administrators to determine what should be done with the news of his suicide. Students and parents in the community wanted to know if the rumors were true. Given the circumstances that Kevin was not a popular student, not well known among mainstream students, and not enrolled at the school at the time of his death, the school decided to down play the incident. It should be noted that this was a time when the contagion effect of suicide was receiving much attention in the media. Therefore, no official announcement was made about Kevin's death to the students or parents. Staff was instructed to just tell anyone who inquired that we were not sure what happened to Kevin, but that the rumors could be true. The special education students who spent a great deal of time with Kevin and the students who attended elementary school with him for six years knew the truth. In fact, they had more details about his death than we did. These students were very troubled by the school's response. He clearly had many problems, but he was a classmate and they had a relationship with him, even if it was a conflicted one. They felt like the school acted as if Kevin did not exist. Most upsetting to them was the feeling of guilt they experienced. Many had confrontations and altercations with Kevin and they mocked him many times. They felt that perhaps they contributed to his problems. Because the school did not acknowledge his death, they could not address the needs of these students. Some wanted to attend his wake and/or funeral, but no information was available. The special education teacher and I reached out to Kevin's classmates in the self-contained class because we knew they would be the most affected by his death. We formed a support group where they could discuss Kevin and express their feelings of regret for what happened to him. They came to understand that his problems were very deep-seeded and that fights among early adolescents are common place; none of this was reason for someone so young to take his life.

If the school had been more honest, it could have put a plan in place to reach out to the many more students who were carrying the same guilt as those students in the self-contained class. By acknowledging his death, the school would have acknowledged his life and allowed a display of public grief for someone who was part of the school system for almost seven years. The act of suicide could have been separated from the person to mitigate the contagion effect, and that would have allowed Kevin to have some dignity in death.

The next student presented a profile that was almost a complete opposite of Kevin's. Hugh was a high school senior who was very well liked by both students and teachers. He was a bright, accomplished student and a key member of the school's drama club. On stage, he presented himself as someone with confidence and poise. Hugh attended a small high school where he was very socially connected and almost everyone knew him. The week before he took his life, he informed me that he was accepted by two of his preferred colleges. Hugh appeared to be on top of the world and no one would have guessed what was about to take place. At a weekend party, he received some bad news from a female friend who he may have had a romantic interest in. He became inebriated at the party but made it home safely with his friends. The next morning, his mother found him hanging in his shower. The principal called all members of the crisis team that day for an early meeting Monday morning. The principal followed the proper protocol by sharing all the factual information as he knew it, and a crisis plan was developed for the day. A faculty meeting immediately followed where the information on Hugh and the crisis plan was shared with staff. The faculty also received some preparation on how students might respond. Tragic news travels fast, especially in a small community, so the vast majority of students knew about Hugh's death. However, they were still informed of the facts during first period. The first few hours were tumultuous as many students were very upset and some of his closest friends were near hysterical in their grief.

As the day progressed, there was talk among the students, especially juniors, as to who might be next in their class. The school had experienced a suicide in the previous graduating class the year before. Consequently, there was an eerie feeling that lightning could strike a third time, and the juniors believed it. The parents also heard this conversation at home and expressed their concern at a meeting held that night for the benefit of the parents. The next day the crisis team met again, and the principal felt pressured to address this issue with the students. The team decided to have a school-wide assembly that day in the auditorium which was to be facilitated by the school psychologist. The goal was to assure students that these events were highly improbable, and that the chances of it happening again were nearly impossible. Also, to mitigate against the "copycat" syndrome, the psychologist would condemn the act itself so students would not see any glory in it. The first part of his presentation went well, but when it came to denouncing the suicide act, the psychologist used very strong language saying that Hugh was stupid for what he did and showed no regard for those who loved him. In the highly charged environment, his friends took offense to the well-meaning psychologist. The girl who Hugh might have had a romantic interest in ran out of the auditorium crying hysterically. His friends began to shout angry responses at the psychologist in defense of their friend. The auditorium became a very chaotic environment with some students screaming while others running out to comfort the student who left earlier. It took some time to calm the students and restore order.

After several stressful days, Hugh's funeral took place, and the school slowly began to return to normal. The school allowed Hugh's friends to memorialize him in student activities and publications, but they wisely refrained from doing anything at school sponsored functions which might appear to glorify him. At such functions, for the remainder of the year, they always paid a respectful moment of silence to remember him.

Fortunately, there were no other suicides in the succeeding years that I was there. There were some very important lessons that all of us learned from Hugh's suicide. One is never to address students on such an emotional topic in a large group setting such as an assembly. The student running out of the auditorium ignited a firestorm of anger towards the psychologist. The emotions initially expressed by his friends became contagious as other students who were not as severely impacted became incensed and angry. In such a large setting, you cannot see body language which may have predicted what was about to happen. Also, you cannot reach out to individual students who may need attention. Another important lesson is that after his death we learned some things about Hugh that even his closest friends did not know: he had made a previous suicide attempt the year before; he was seeing a therapist at the time of his death; he had serious anger management problems which was compounded by frequent drinking; his mother was a lesbian and he may have been having some sexual identity problems. On the surface, he seemed very well adjusted and happy. Obviously, this was not the case. While these matters are private and knowing these things may not have made a difference, I believe the school and those who knew him best may have been more observant and attentive if they knew he was at risk. Clearly, sharing some of this information is a personal decision and the parent must have a level of trust that the school will act in their child's best interest.

The last case also deals with a high school senior. Tom had a very different and distinctive profile than both Kevin and Hugh. He lived with his mother and sister in a house only two blocks from the school. Tom was an average student who had a passion for art. He took many of his electives in art and was in AP Art his senior year. His social network was somewhat limited; he tended to socialize with a close group of peers, many of whom were also "artsy" and formed their own subgroup in the school. His art teacher, who knew him well, did have some concerns about his moodiness. At times he seemed fine, but other times he was depressed. This is often the case with many teenagers. For the most part, he seemed to function academically, socially, and behaviorally with some occasional transgressions.

One early spring morning, some teachers driving to school noticed police cars in front of Tom's house. As the school day began, the principal received a phone call from the police department reporting that Tom had been found dead in his home from a gunshot wound. At that point, there was no confirmation that it was self-inflicted. The principal immediately convened a meeting of the crisis team. A plan for notifying the faculty and students was developed. The school day had already begun, so there was no way that we could have a faculty meeting to notify the teachers. Therefore, the crisis team members took it upon themselves to notify teachers throughout the building individually. Those who were in class teaching were informed at the end of the period. One important point to note here is that although a suicide was strongly suspected, the police made no mention of suicide. Therefore, the message to every teacher had to be that he died of a gunshot wound without any further explanation. The next step involved notifying the students. The juniors and seniors had open campus privileges, and many would be leaving school grounds during their lunch period. The team felt that it was important that they be notified before the first lunch period. Otherwise, they would find out about Tom through the rumors spreading around the community. Also, of even greater concern, should the school announce such tragic news and then let the juniors and seniors leave the building? How can faculty monitor students who are seriously impacted by the news if they are not in the building? A statement was prepared by the crisis team that was read to each class. The upperclassmen were the most impacted by the news, and many students were crying. The pupil personnel staff tried its best to reach out to both students and teachers who were obviously upset. The team would have preferred to keep all students inside that day, but there was not enough time to deal with all the logistics of accommodating all the juniors and seniors in the cafeteria. The principal decided to let them go out to lunch. Some students did not return after lunch. Perhaps the saddest moment in the aftermath of Tom's death was when several of Tom's friends were escorted into my office because they were crying hysterically. They related that Tom had emailed them a few weeks ago threatening to kill himself. As good friends do, they tried to help him. They drove to his house, picked him up in their car, and spoke to him. When they dropped him off at home, he seemed calmer and for the next few days at school, he seemed better. They thought his depression had lifted. These friends never told anyone of the incident, and now they were feeling extremely guilty. They never realized how troubled Tom was, and by not reporting the incident they missed an opportunity to save him.

The next few days were terrible as the school struggled to support its grieving students and staff. The police confirmed that it was a suicide and the students and parents were kept updated as to the latest information. Because the tragedy occurred on a Friday, the crisis team kept the school open over the weekend so that counselors would be available to speak to students and parents. The fear of the suicide contagion was not as great in this case. His death was clearly not glorified, and he did not have enough of a social following to be a role model for other students who were fragile like himself. Nonetheless, important lessons were learned in the wake of Tom's death.

Perhaps the biggest lesson is that students need to be better educated on what to do when a friend expresses suicidal intentions. As a result of Tom's death, an activity was introduced in our freshman transition program. The program seeks to assist 9th graders with their transition to high school. At one of these meetings, a copy of the email that Tom wrote to his friends is distributed to the freshman and they are asked: What would you do if you receive this email from a friend? It is interesting to see how some students still regard reporting the incident as a betrayal of a friend. After sharing the tragedy of Tom's death, all realize the importance of reporting such information with an adult.

Given the timing of his death, the crisis team responded quickly, developing and implementing a reasonably effective crisis plan. However, the school took a real risk in permitting upperclassmen to leave the school grounds for lunch so soon after receiving the news. Fortunately, there were no negative consequences. Today, most schools have a mass email system for notifying parents, which should be used in this situation. An email could be sent to the parents informing them of the incident and asking their permission to release students from the building for lunch. Only those students whose parents give permission would be allowed to leave the building.

The American Foundation for Suicide Prevention is an organization that offers excellent resources to schools for preventing suicide. The AFSP was founded as a non-profit organization in 1987 by a group of scientists who were concerned about the rising rates of suicide in this country. While its original mission is still to conduct research on the causes of suicide, it has developed some wonderful educational programs for schools including training programs for mental health professionals, teachers, and other educators. Through its research, the organization maintains the most current information on statistics and suicide trends among different age groups. The AFSP has also created educational films for high school and college students on the causes and warning signs of suicide, and will also visit schools to speak to students. Services are also provided to the family and other loved ones which include support groups and a yearly conference where survivors can share their experiences. Most of its activities are supported through fundraising events, the most famous of which are "Out of the Darkness" walks that are held throughout the country. The walks also serve an important public service by educating its participants on issues related to suicide. The AFSP can be accessed through its website, afsp.org.

CONCLUSION: IT TAKES A VILLAGE

In Hillary Clinton's book, she describes changes in our society which have transformed families. The extended family, living in the same geographic area with several adults to provide stability and nurturance for the children, has been replaced by the nuclear family. She explains how the urbanization of America and the need for mobility in our rapidly changing society has created many nuclear families where both parents work. Consequently, children often have to fend for themselves for a good part of the day. Furthermore, the high divorce rate and prevalence of single parent homes have further eroded parental influence. Raising children has become a communal effort where teachers, child care providers, police, clergy, and neighbors, as well as parents have all become partners. This concept is well illustrated by a family that I have been recently working with. The father of this family died, leaving behind his wife and two daughters. The overwhelmed and financially distressed mother needed to find help for her daughters. She tried to seek out a support group for teenagers in her area. She contacted the schools they attended, parish-based programs in her community, and local mental health centers. Much to her chagrin, none of these resources had a support group for adolescents. She ultimately turned to me for private counseling for the younger daughter. Much of her day is spent driving her daughters to school-related functions or after school activities. In between her various car trips, she has to find time to look for a job. Just to find a convenient time to make a counseling appointment with her daughter was difficult. It was sad to see how this devoted mother was so alone in providing for the needs of her family.

As stated in Hillary's book, the decline of the extended family has left many families more isolated with fewer individuals that they can turn to for help. Therefore, they look to other resources in the child's environment. Schools are well positioned to provide this valuable support since students spend more time in school than any other place outside of their home. Community mental health programs are hampered by the transportation needs of their clients making adolescent support groups less viable. While schools are the best venue to providing this service, they face a formidable challenge. Politicians and educational leaders are so obsessed with raising academic standards that other important needs are being ignored. Teenagers are not going to perform at a high academic level if they are struggling with the emotional turmoil of grief. How is a standardized test going to accurately measure a grieving student's math or reading proficiency? Therefore, school administrators need to support school mental health professionals in this important endeavor.

Working with newly bereaved youngsters does not require advanced degrees in clinical psychology. Graduate programs in school counseling, social work, and psychology already provide these professionals with the needed skill set to facilitate groups. Professional development workshops can provide a deeper understanding of the psychodynamics of grief that is needed to counsel newly bereaved adolescents and to facilitate bereavement support groups.

Similarly, in cases where there is the death of a student in a school, a communal effort is required. There are many resources in most communities that can be called upon to assist the school and the family. In these crises, it truly takes a village and we all need to become caregivers and stakeholders in the future of our children.

NOTES

(Endnotes)

1. Parkes, C.M. <u>Bereavement : Studies in Grief in Adult Life</u>, N.Y.: International Universities Press, 1972, p. 23.
2. Lorenz, K. <u>On Aggression</u>. London: Methuen, 1963, p.208.
3. McGoldrick, M & Walsh, F. <u>Living Beyond Loss</u>. New York: W.W. Norton, 2004, p. 141
4. McGoldrick, M & Walsh, F. <u>Living Beyond Loss</u>. New York: W.W. Norton, 2004, p. 145
5. McGoldrick, M & Walsh, F. <u>Living Beyond Loss</u>. New York: W.W. Norton, 2004, p. 137
6. McGoldrick, M & Walsh, F. <u>Living Beyond Loss</u>. New York: W.W. Norton, 2004, p. 122
7. Doka, K.J. & Martin, T.L. Take It Like a Man: Understanding Masculine Grief, <u>Caregivers Quarterly</u>, 1997, 12:2, p.2
8. Worden, J.W. <u>Grief Counseling and Grief Therapy</u> (4th ed.) New York: Springer, 2009, p. 231-233
9. Hogan, N.S. & DeSantis L. Adolescent Sibling Bereavement: An Ongoing Sibling Attachment, <u>Qualitative Health Research</u>, 1992, 2:2, p. 171-173
10. Hogan, N.S. & DeSantis L. Things That Help and Hinder Adolescent Sibling Bereavement, <u>Western Journal of Nursing Research</u>, 1994, 16:2, p. 137-141

REFERENCES

Bonanno. G. The Other Side of Sadness. N.Y.: Basic Books, 2009

Clinton, H. It Takes a Village. N.Y.: Simon & Schuster, 1996.

Crenshaw, D.A. Bereavement. N.Y.: Crossroad Publishing Co., 1999.

Doka, K.J. & Martin, T.L. Take It Like a Man: Understanding Masculine Grief, Caregivers Quarterly, 1997.

Freud, S. Mourning and Melancholia. In J. Strachey (Ed. & Trans.) The standard edition of the complete psychological works of Sigmund Freud (Vol. 14, pp 237-260) London: Hogarth. (Originally published in 1917).

Frankl, V.E. Man's search for Meaning. Boston: Beacon Press, 1959.

Gray, J. Men are from Mars, Women are from Venus. N.Y.: Harper Collins, 1992.

Grollman, E.A. Straight Talk About Death For Teenagers. Boston: Beacon Press, 1993.

Hogan, N.S. & DeSantis L. Adolescent Sibling Bereavement: An Ongoing Sibling Attachment, Qualitative Health Research, 1992, 2:2, p. 159-177.

Hogan, N.S. & DeSantis L. Things That Help and Hinder Adolescent Sibling Bereavement, Western Journal of Nursing Research, 1994, 16:2, p. 132-153.

Kubler-Ross, E. On Death and Dying. N.Y.: MacMillan, 1969.

Lehman, L., Jimerson, S.R. & Gaasch, A. Teens Together Grief
    Support Group Curriculum, N.Y.: Taylor & Francis, 2001.

Lorenz, K. On Agression London: Methuen, 1963.

McGoldrick, M & Walsh, F. Living Beyond Loss. New York: W.W.
    Norton, 2004.

Parkes, C.M. Bereavement : Studies in Grief in Adult Life, N.Y.:
    International Universities Press, 1972.

Riethmayer, J. Living with Loss Bryan, Texas: BJR Enterprises,
    1992.

Stroebe, M.S. & Schut, H The Dual Process Model of Coping with
    Bereavement: Rationale and Description Death Studies, 1999,
    23:3, P. 197-224.

Wolfelt, A. Helping Children Cope with Grief, Muncie, IN:
    Accelerated Development, Inc. 1983.

Worden, J.W. Grief Counseling and Grief Therapy (4th ed.) New
    York: Springer, 2009.

ABOUT THE AUTHOR

As a middle school counselor in the early 1980's, Luciano Sabatini went through a very personal and painful experience. His wife and high school sweetheart Linda died after a long bout with cancer. During this tumultuous time, he struggled to cope with his grief and to accept her death. Perhaps the most difficult part of the grieving process was trying to understand why someone so young, innocent, and full of life had to die. All he had left of Linda were memories. As he began to heal, he decided to try to find some meaning to this tragedy. With the wisdom he had gained from his own grief, he decided to reach out to and help other widowed individuals. By helping others, perhaps something good could come from her death.

Working as a volunteer for the American Red Cross, he began to facilitate bereavement support groups for men. During this time he did a doctoral research study through Columbia Pacific University on the effectiveness of support groups in treating grief, and eventually earned a Ph.D. in Counseling Psychology.

After a few years, he decided to venture on his own and started a parish based bereavement program where he facilitates support groups, trains individuals who were interested in helping the newly bereaved, offers private counseling and conducts numerous workshops on topics related to grief.

Working in school settings, his interest in bereavement counseling expanded when he participated on crisis teams formed to help schools deal with crises such as the death of a student. He began to work with newly bereaved students individually and then progressed to facilitating support groups for students who had lost a loved one.

In over 25 years as a bereavement counselor, he has assisted hundreds of bereaved adults and adolescents in dealing with their grief. He recently retired from secondary education but continues with his work as a bereavement counselor. He is currently an adjunct professor at Hofstra University where he teaches a graduate course, "Counseling for Death, Dying and Bereavement" on alternate summers in the school counseling program.

Luciano also serves as a consultant to funeral homes, schools, parish bereavement programs and community organizations.

For further information, please visit his website, www. empoweringthebereaved.com or email him at lousab@aol.com

CPSIA information can be obtained at www.ICGtesting.com
Printed in the USA
BVOW07s1848311013

335174BV00003B/127/P